Already Whole

Unlock The Eight Keys to Emotional Freedom and Inner Peace

Elijah Kai

Copyright © 2025 Elijah Kai

All rights reserved. No part of this publication may be reproduced, distributed, or transmitted in any form or by any means, including photocopying, recording, or other electronic or mechanical methods, without the prior written permission of the publisher, except in the case of brief quotations embodied in critical reviews and certain other noncommercial uses permitted by copyright law. For permission requests, write to the publisher addressed, "Attention: Permission Request," at Elijah@belieftheory.com

DISCLAIMER: This is a work of nonfiction. Nonetheless, some of the names and identifying character traits of people featured in the stories herein have been changed in order to protect their identities (including stories used with the subject's full permission). Any resulting resemblance to persons either living or dead is entirely coincidental.

ISBN: 9798309937738

First edition: February 2025

Written by Elijah Kai
Published by Elijah Kai
Front and back cover design by Kamene Bacon

Dedication

To you—

The one who has spent a lifetime searching for something you can't quite name. The one who has carried burdens in silence, who has tried to hold it all together, who has wondered if peace was something meant for everyone except you.

I wrote this for you.

Not to give you anything you don't already have, but to remind you of what has always been yours. You don't have to try so hard. You don't have to keep proving, fixing, chasing.

You are already whole. And when you finally see it for yourself, everything changes.

Thank you for being here. Thank you for trusting me with your time, your heart, your openness. Out of all the books, all the words, all the ways you could have spent this moment—you chose to be here.

I honor you for that.
I see you.
I am grateful for you and I love you.

May this book serve you in ways beyond what you expected.

Acknowledgments

This book is not just my work—it's a reflection of every soul who has touched my life and led me to this moment.

To my clients, who trusted me with their stories, their pain, and their breakthroughs—you are the reason this book exists. Your courage, your willingness to step into the unknown, and your commitment to your own healing inspires me every single day.

To Hank, the man who interrupted my pattern at 20 years old—your impact on my life is immeasurable. And to Sergeant Hawkins, who saw something in me when I couldn't yet see it in myself—you changed my path forever.

To Steve Hardison, your unwavering belief in human potential and your example of *being* have left an indelible mark on my life. And to Townsend Wardlaw, who introduced me to Steve and helped me shatter layers of epigenetic and cultural limitations—I am forever grateful.

To my brothers and sisters in this work—Michael Jaimes, D.B. Bedford, Judy and Erik Thureson, Esther Alley, Alok Appadurai, Seth Pepper, Sanyika Firestarter, Kusudi Muithi and Andre Norman—your wisdom, friendship, and presence have been gifts beyond measure.

To my wife, Kamene, my daughter, Kaia, my son, Kristian, my son's mother, Kristine, my parents, Steven Bacon Sr. and Ramona Lofton, and my surrogate parents who have adopted me as their son—you are my greatest teachers. You remind me, every day, of what it truly means to love, to be present, and to grow.

To my past self—thank you for never giving up. For choosing, again and again, to keep going, to seek truth, and to trust in something greater than what you could see.

And to every single person I haven't named here, but whose presence has shaped me in ways I may never even fully understand—I honor you.

This book was never just mine. It belongs to all of us. Thank you.

Table of Contents

Dedication	i
Acknowledgments	ii
INTRODUCTION	1
The Journey Back To Yourself	
CHAPTER 1	7
What Are You Striving For?	
CHAPTER 2	27
What Are You Avoiding?	
CHAPTER 3	37
Putting The Game Of Life On Hard	
CHAPTER 4	48
You Are Not Who You Think You Are	
CHAPTER 5	59
Coping Vs. Healing	
CHAPTER 6	67
The Eight Keys To Emotional Freedom	
CHAPTER 7	73
Key # 1: It Wasn't About You	
CHAPTER 8	83
Key #2: It Had Nothing To Do With You	
CHAPTER 9	94
Key #3: It Was None Of Your Business	
CHAPTER 10	106
Key #4: Everyone Is Doing The Best They Can With The Mind And Resources They Have At The Time	

CHAPTER 11   117

Key #5: You Were Loved, Just Not The Way You Wanted To Be Loved

CHAPTER 12   132

Key #6: All Human Behavior Is Motivated By Positive Intent (Just Not For Everyone Involved)

CHAPTER 13   144

Key #7: We Judge Others By Their Actions, Ourselves By Our Intentions

CHAPTER 14   169

Key #8: Respect Other People's Way Of Seeing The World (Even If You Don't Understand It)

CHAPTER 15   187

The Bridge Between Healing And Wholeness

CHAPTER 16   192

You Are Not Your Thoughts Or Your Identity

CHAPTER 17   208

Becoming Childlike Again

CHAPTER 18   222

Emotional Enlightenment

CONCLUSION   237

Your New Journey Begins Here

Introduction

The Journey Back to Yourself

Take a deep breath. You made it. That might not seem like much, but it is.

Because in this moment, with everything else going on in your life, you made a decision to be here—to open this book, to explore something deeper, to see if maybe, just maybe, there's another way to feel at peace. That says a lot.

I don't know exactly what brought you here. Maybe you've tried everything—therapy, coaching, self-help books—and yet, something still feels off. Like there's a missing piece you just can't seem to find.

Or maybe you've achieved everything you thought would make you happy—success, relationships, accomplishments—but it still doesn't feel like enough. You're standing at the top of the mountain you spent your whole life climbing, and yet, deep down, there's still this quiet ache inside.

And maybe you can't even put words to it. Maybe all you know is that you feel stuck, restless, or tired in a way that sleep doesn't fix. Whatever it is, I want you to know this, **you are not broken**. There is nothing wrong with you. **You are already whole.**

I know that might be hard to believe. I know the world has told you otherwise. But that's why this book exists.

This Book Is for You—No Matter Your Story

I need you to hear this before we go any further. This book is for you, no matter what your life has looked like.

You might read some of the stories later in this book—stories of trauma, pain, and survival—and think, *"Well, my life hasn't been that bad. Maybe this isn't for me."*

Or maybe you'll feel the opposite. Maybe you'll think, *"My pain runs deeper than anything in these pages. Nothing can undo what I've been through."* Either way, I promise you—you are exactly where you need to be.

This book isn't about comparing pain or measuring wounds. It's about freedom—from whatever has been weighing on you. For some, that weight is trauma. For others, it's the silent pressure to always be achieving. For others, it's the feeling of never quite being enough—no matter what they do.

Whatever it is for you, I want you to know you are not alone in this. You don't have to carry it forever. And no matter how heavy it feels right now, emotional freedom and inner peace are possible for you. That's what the **Eight Keys** are about. They aren't just ideas—they are a pathway back to yourself. A way to remove the layers of fear, guilt, shame, and limiting beliefs that have kept you from seeing the truth. You don't need fixing. You don't need to become someone new.

You just need to remember who you really are.

Why I Wrote This Book

I didn't always know this truth. For years, I carried my own weight—more than I thought I could bear. My childhood was filled with instability, trauma, and survival. I experienced things no child should—moving through crack houses, being molested, almost kidnapped, shuffled through 14 different schools, and struggling with the feeling that I had to be someone else just to survive.

By the time I was 23, I had already hit rock bottom—two failed marriages, homelessness, and a felony on my record. I was angry, lost, and destructive to the people who cared about me. For most of my life, I thought I was too far gone.

Until one day, I wasn't.

I met someone who introduced me to personal development. That moment cracked open a door I didn't even know existed—a world where healing, growth, and transformation were possible.

I threw myself into it. I read every book I could find, listened to the greats like Tony Robbins and Les Brown, attended retreats and seminars, and eventually became a certified master in Neuro-Linguistic Programming (NLP). Slowly but surely, I started healing—rebuilding my life, repairing my relationships, and learning how to change the beliefs that had been running my life.

And in that process, I discovered something life-changing: I wasn't broken. **I was already whole**.

Everything I had been chasing—peace, confidence, love, worthiness—was never outside of me. It was buried under layers of pain, survival, and false beliefs. I didn't need to become someone new. I just needed to unlearn everything that wasn't me.

The Journey We're About to Take

This book is written as a conversation between us. Not as a teacher to a student. Not as an expert to a beginner. But as someone who has walked this road, sitting next to you, guiding you back home to yourself.

Over the next chapters, I'll share the **Eight Keys** to Emotional Freedom—the same keys that helped me, my clients, and hundreds of others experience peace, clarity, and deep transformation. But I need you to know—this book isn't just about emotional healing.

It's about something even bigger.
At a certain point in this journey, something shifts. You stop identifying with your past. You stop chasing peace and realize you are peace. You stop seeking happiness and see that you are happiness itself. This is where true freedom begins—not just from emotional baggage, but from the illusion that you were ever anything less than whole.

This book isn't just about healing your past. It's about waking up to who you really are. So, if you're willing to trust this process, if you're open to something deeper than self-improvement, I promise you—this will change the way you see yourself forever.

How to Read This Book

This isn't the kind of book you rush through. It's not a book you skim, looking for quick answers. It's a book that meets you exactly where you are—whether you're just starting your journey of self-discovery, or you've been walking this path for years.

Some parts will resonate deeply. Others might challenge you. Some chapters might unlock something in you immediately, while others might not fully land until weeks, months, or even years later.

That's okay. This book is meant to be experienced—not just read.

So, here's my advice:
- **Take your time.** Let the words sink in. Pause when you need to. Revisit chapters that speak to you.
- **Pay attention to what stirs inside you.** If something triggers an emotion—lean in. That's where your freedom is waiting.
- **Let yourself be uncomfortable.** Growth isn't always easy. Some of these concepts might feel unfamiliar or even challenge long-held beliefs. That's part of the process.
- **Don't just think—feel.** This isn't a book to be analyzed like a textbook. It's an invitation to be present with yourself in a new way.

And most importantly:
- **Trust yourself.** There's no "right" way to read this book—only the way that feels right for you.

If a passage speaks to you, sit with it. If a story doesn't seem to apply to your life, look beyond the details to the deeper truth. The words in these pages aren't about me or the people whose stories I share. **They're about you.** This is your journey. And you get to take it at your own pace.

How to Get the Most from This Book

There's something powerful about not just reading transformational ideas but actually living them.

Here's how to get the most out of this book:
- **Read with an open heart, not just an open mind.** Some of the biggest breakthroughs come when you let go of intellectual understanding and just allow yourself to experience what's being said.
- **Reflect on your own life as you go.** This isn't about theory—it's about you. As you read, ask yourself: *"Where have I seen this pattern in my own life? How has this belief shaped my decisions? What would change if I let this go?"*
- **Engage with the Eight Keys like a practice, not just a concept.** Transformation isn't about knowing something—it's about living it. The **Eight Keys** are here to be applied, not just understood.
- **Return to this book whenever you need it.** Healing isn't linear. You might feel amazing one day and struggle the next. That's normal. Let this book be a guide you can return to anytime you need clarity.

And above all…
- **Be gentle with yourself.** This isn't about "getting it right." There is no test at the end. There is only **you**, meeting yourself in new ways, discovering what's been waiting inside you all along.

A Personal Invitation to Go Deeper

This journey doesn't have to end when you close this book.

If something in these pages speaks to you—if it awakens a curiosity, a knowing, or a hunger for more—you don't have to figure it all out alone.

I invite you to experience the **Eight Keys** in a live workshop, retreat, or personal coaching session. There's something powerful about being in a room with others on the same path—where transformation becomes real in ways that can't always happen on the page. Visit: www.The8keys.com or reach out to me directly at elijah@belieftheory.com

And if you ever need someone to speak to your team, organization, or community, I'd be honored to share these principles in a way that resonates with your group.

This is more than a book. **It's a movement.**

And I'd love for you to be a part of it.

Chapter 1

What Are You Striving For?

It Was Never About the Goal

Let's be honest—you thought it would feel different by now, didn't you? You worked hard. You did everything you were supposed to do. Maybe you built a career, raised a family, earned degrees, or hit that financial number you thought would finally bring peace. On the outside, it looks like you've got it all. People admire you. But inside, there's a quiet ache.

Even with all the accomplishments, there's a voice whispering, *"this isn't it. Why don't I feel better?"* No matter what you achieve, it never feels like enough. You told yourself that the next achievement would do it. The next promotion, the perfect relationship, the dream house. But here you are, still wondering, *"Why do I feel this way?"*

You might even find yourself thinking, *"Maybe I missed something along the way."* You look at others—your colleagues, friends, the people on social media—and wonder if they've figured it out. They look happy, fulfilled. And here you are, holding everything you've ever wanted in your hands, wondering why it still feels like something's missing.

You've probably tried to brush it off, telling yourself, *"I should just be grateful."* But deep down, you know that quiet ache isn't going away. Gratitude feels like a mask you put on to convince yourself everything's fine. And it feels like no one around you understands. You feel like you're running a race with no finish line—one goal after the next, never quite arriving. And it's exhausting.

Have you ever paused to wonder if the reason it feels this way isn't because you haven't done enough, but because it was never about the goal in the first place? Was it ever about the title, the degree, the money or the achievement? Were those just placeholders for something deeper like a longing for peace, meaning or a sense of being enough just as you are?

When you build your life chasing those placeholders, you're left feeling like you're pouring water into a bottomless cup. It doesn't matter how much you pour—the emptiness remains. The goals might give you a moment of satisfaction, but it fades as quickly as it comes. And before you know it, you're back at square one, setting another goal, chasing another dream, hoping this time it'll be different.

And if we're being really honest, you've probably tried to silence that ache with distractions. Whether it's the grind of work, the escape of vacations, or numbing it out with food, alcohol, or scrolling your phone late at night. It's easier to keep moving than to stop and feel because stopping means facing the truth: The life you've built isn't filling the void.

But here's the good news: You're not alone. I know this ache because I've lived it. I've stood at the top of my "mountain", looked out at everything I thought would bring me peace, and realized I still felt empty inside. And if you're here, reading these words, it means you're ready to stop running. You're ready to face that ache and find the peace that's been eluding you.

The problem isn't that you haven't achieved enough. The problem is that you've been looking for peace in all the wrong places. The peace you're looking for isn't out there—it's already within you.

So, let's pause. Take a deep breath. And let's explore the ache together. Because what you're feeling isn't failure—it's an invitation.

You probably don't talk about this ache with anyone. Maybe it feels too personal, or maybe you're afraid they wouldn't understand. You've built a life that looks so good on the outside—who would even believe you feel this way? How do you explain that the success you worked so hard for—the life you dreamed about—isn't filling the space inside you?

I see you.

I see the quiet war you fight every day, the battle between the face you show the world and the doubts that swirl in your mind when no one's watching. You've built something people admire. They look at you and think you've figured it all out. And maybe you've let them think that because what else are you supposed to do? But when the room is quiet, when it's just you and your thoughts, there it is—that ache. That nagging feeling that no matter what you accomplish, no matter how much you check off the list, something's missing.

You've tried to fill the space, haven't you? You've turned to self-help books, podcasts, therapy, coaching—searching for something to quiet that voice that says, *"This isn't it."* And maybe some of it worked. Maybe you found moments of relief. But then, just as quickly as it left, that ache came back.

And I know you've wondered, *"What's wrong with me? Why do I feel this way when I've done everything I was supposed to do?"*

Let me tell you something right now. There's nothing wrong with you. That ache you feel? That's not failure. That's not brokenness. It's something else entirely—it's a signal.

What if that ache isn't a sign of failure, but a whisper from your soul? Could it be nudging you toward something deeper—a truer way of living and being? What if it's not about what you've done wrong; but about what you've outgrown?

Think of it like wearing shoes that no longer fit. At first, you don't notice the discomfort. You keep walking because that's what you've always done. But eventually, the pinch becomes unbearable. That ache you feel? It's the pinch. It's a sign that the life you've built, as impressive as it looks, isn't spacious enough for who you've become.

The problem isn't you—it's the rules you've been following, the story you've been living by. The one that says if you just work harder, achieve more, earn more, love better—you'll finally feel at peace. But peace doesn't come from working harder or achieving more.

You've done all that, haven't you? You've climbed the mountain, only to find that the view didn't bring the peace you expected. That ache you feel is your wake-up call, not your failure. It's your soul saying, *there's more*. It's a call to look inward, to uncover the stories and emotions shaping your life so that you can reclaim your peace.

A Life Built for Applause

Does your life look amazing on the outside, but somewhere along the way, you lost sight of what feels good to you? Maybe your achievements became more about proving something than experiencing something.

Does this sound familiar?

- You hit a milestone, but instead of celebrating, you immediately set a new goal because stopping feels too risky.
- You give so much of yourself to everyone else—your team, your family, your community—but when it comes to your own needs, you feel selfish even thinking about them.
- You've built walls to protect yourself from the pain you've experienced, but those same walls are keeping out the joy and connection you crave.
- You've been running so hard, chasing the next thing, that you haven't had time to stop and ask yourself, *"What am I really after?"*

The Whisper of Truth

If you're honest, you've heard the whisper of truth beneath all the noise. It's quiet, but it's there. It's the voice that says, *"You were made for more than this."* Not more achievements, not more accolades, but more peace, more freedom, more you.

You're not alone in this. The ache you feel? It's part of the human experience, especially for those who've reached the heights you have. The reason this emptiness stays with you no matter what you achieve is because *you can never get enough of what you didn't need in the first place.* **You're not broken**—you're awakening. You're being called to let go of the old story, the one that got you this far but can't take you any further.

I see you. And I want you to see yourself, not as someone who's failed to find peace, but as someone standing on the edge of a breakthrough.

The First 14 Years: The Silent Story That Shapes Everything

You might not think about it much—those early years of your life—but they've shaped you in ways you can't imagine. By the time you were 14, the foundation for how you see yourself and the world around you were already laid. The beliefs you hold about what's possible, what you're worthy of, and how you fit into the grand scheme of life? Those were planted long before you became the accomplished adult sitting here today.

Think about that for a moment. Before you could drive a car or legally sign your name, the blueprint for your life was already drawn. And unless you've actively revisited and reprogrammed those beliefs, they're still running the show.

It's not just the big, obvious things—like a chaotic household or a traumatic event. It's also the quiet, subtle moments that shaped your perception.

Maybe it was a single moment—a look, a word, or a silence—that planted a seed of doubt about your worth. Maybe it was the way a teacher's offhand comment stuck with you or the way you felt invisible at home unless you were excelling. Perhaps it was the tension in the air during a fight you didn't understand but felt deeply.

Whatever your experience was, your brain, like a sponge, absorbed everything. But as kids, we don't process these moments with logic or nuance. Everything feels personal. If your parents argued about money, you might've thought, *I'm a burden*. If a parent left, you might've decided, *I wasn't good enough to make them stay*. If love felt conditional, you might've believed, *I have to work hard to earn my place in the world*.

Those conclusions, those childlike interpretations, weren't made with wisdom or foresight. They were survival strategies—your best attempt to make sense of a confusing world. They worked back then, but now? They've become invisible walls, quietly dictating what you believe you're capable of and what you think you deserve.

The Child Running the Show

Imagine this, you've built an incredible life—an empire, a career, a family—but every decision still has to go through an eight-year-old version of you. That child decides how you respond to criticism, handle conflict, and even how much joy you allow yourself to feel.

These early beliefs didn't disappear when you grew up; they went underground, silently shaping how you think, feel, and act. They weren't conscious choices—they were survival strategies you developed as a child to feel safe, loved, and accepted. The problem? Those strategies were built for a different time and place, and now they're running your adult life in ways you might not even realize.

For example, think about how you react in a meeting when someone critiques your idea. Instead of seeing it as feedback, you feel small, like you did something wrong. Your mind spirals: *They think I'm a failure. I don't belong here.* That's the child inside you, responding to an old fear of not being good enough.

Or maybe, during a disagreement, your partner says something hurtful. Instead of addressing it calmly, you withdraw emotionally or lash out in anger. That's not the adult you—it's the child, trying to protect themselves the only way they know how.

These patterns play out everywhere—in boardrooms, relationships, and goals—because the rules of your childhood survival strategies still govern your behavior. They've become so ingrained that they feel like your personality. But in reality, they're outdated software that keeps you stuck.

Take The Overachiever, for example. As a child, you might've learned that earning your worth through achievement was the only way to feel valuable. Now, you're the one taking on every project, working endless hours, and never feeling like you've done enough—even when others admire your success.

Or consider The People-Pleaser. Maybe love in your childhood came with strings attached, so you learned to prioritize everyone else's needs, leaving little for yourself. Today, you say yes to everything, even when it drains you.

Then, there's The Lone Wolf. Growing up in chaos, you may have told yourself, *I can't count on anyone*. Now, that belief shows up as a reluctance to trust others, delegate, or let your guard down—even in relationships.

Here's the irony, these strategies often look like strengths to the outside world. People praise your work ethic, your independence, your generosity. But inside, they come with an invisible cost: burnout, isolation, and a nagging sense that something's missing.

The truth is, the life you've built is bigger than these survival strategies. You don't need the old rules anymore—they served you back then, but now they're holding you back. It's time to stop letting an eight-year-old run the show and start reclaiming your peace.

The Case for Revisiting the First 14 Years

If you've ever wondered why success doesn't feel like enough, why your relationships hit the same roadblocks, or why peace seems so elusive, this is why.

It's not because something is wrong with you. It's because the blueprint you're working from was designed for a time when survival was your only goal. And the beliefs that helped you survive as a child are now holding you back as an adult.

This isn't about fixing yourself—**you're not broken**. It's about recognizing that the stories running your life were written by a child who didn't have the full picture. It's about seeing those stories for what they are: outdated software that needs an upgrade.

Let me be clear, the strength that got you here—the resilience, the determination, the ability to push forward—came from those early stories. But imagine what could happen if you weren't carrying that old weight anymore.

What if you could make decisions from a place of freedom instead of fear? What if you could stop running and start living?

This isn't about reliving pain or blaming anyone. It's about looking at those first 14 years with fresh eyes, recognizing the beliefs you've outgrown, and deciding to let them go.

Because the truth is, you are not the story you've been living by. You are so much more.

Survival Strategies That Became Your Identity

As kids, we're wired to survive. Our number one goal isn't to thrive—it's to feel safe, loved, and accepted. And when those things feel uncertain, we adapt. We become whatever we need to be to get by. The trouble is, those strategies don't just disappear when we grow up. They get baked into our identity, silently shaping how we show up in the world.

You might not think of yourself as someone "playing it safe" or "adapting to survive." After all, you've built a life most people dream of. But here's the twist: the very strengths that got you here might be rooted in childhood strategies you haven't outgrown. They served you back then, but today, they could be keeping you from the deeper fulfillment you're craving.

Kids don't have the tools to analyze their world objectively. They see everything in black and white, and they make sense of life through a simple lens: What do I need to do to feel safe and loved?

That question led you to develop behaviors and beliefs tailored to your environment. If love was conditional, you might've become a perfectionist, thinking, *"If I just get everything right, they'll love me."* If chaos ruled your home, you might've become hyper-independent, telling yourself, *"I can't rely on anyone else—I have to handle this on my own."*

Again, these weren't conscious choices. They were your best attempts to navigate life with the limited understanding you had. And the strategies worked—so well, in fact, that they became second nature. They became your default way of operating.

Those survival strategies weren't built for the life you're living now. They were designed to get you through childhood, but they don't fit the challenges you face as an adult. They're like outdated armor—heavy, restrictive, and unnecessary for the battles you're fighting today.

Take The Overachiever, for example. In childhood, striving for perfection might've won you love or approval. But now? It keeps you stuck in a loop of never feeling good enough. Or The Lone Wolf—self-reliance kept you safe back then, but now it might be stopping you from building the connections you crave.

These strategies don't make you weak or flawed. They're proof of how resourceful you were as a kid. But as an adult, they're like running a marathon with weights on your ankles. The very things that helped you survive are now keeping you from the emotional freedom and inner peace you are longing for.

Here's what makes these survival strategies so tricky, they're not obvious. They don't announce themselves as "childhood coping mechanisms." They feel like you. Like your personality. Your habits. Your strengths. That's why they're so hard to spot—and even harder to let go of.

Think about it:

- Why do you overcommit, even when you know it'll burn you out?
- Why does criticism hit you harder than it should?
- Why do you struggle to let people in, even when you want deeper connections?

The answer isn't because you're broken. It's because an old rule—written by a much younger version of you—is still running the show. That child decided what you needed to do to feel safe, and you've been following those rules ever since without question.

Just because these strategies shaped you doesn't mean they have to define you. You can rewrite the rules. You can trade survival for freedom.

But first, you have to recognize the strategies for what they are. They're not flaws. They're not failures. They're reminders of how adaptive, resilient, and resourceful you were. And now, it's time to honor those strategies—and gently let them go.

The truth is, the life you've built is bigger than the survival strategies that got you here. And the freedom you're looking for? It's already within you. You just need to take off the armor.

The Courtroom of an Eight-Year-Old

Imagine a courtroom where the Judge is eight years old, the prosecutor is eight years old, the eye witness is eight years old and the jury are all eight-year-olds. There's no defense attorney or cross examinations allowed and you're the one on trial. How fair of a trial would that be? No one to argue your case or present the bigger picture. Just a scared, overwhelmed child making rulings based on limited evidence, high emotions, and a complete lack of context.

That's what your early years were like. In this courtroom, you were both the accused and the one handing out verdicts. Every moment—every argument, every silence, every glance—was put on trial. And with the limited understanding of a child, you ruled on what those moments meant about you, your worth, and your place in the world.

- A dad walked out the door and didn't come back? The child thinks, "*I must not be lovable.*"
- A mom was too tired to listen? The child says, "*I'm a burden.*"
- A teacher scolded you for speaking up in class? The child believes, "*I need to stay quiet to be safe.*"

Without a mature adult defense attorney to argue for your value or a wise adult judge to provide perspective, those childhood conclusions became your truth. And once the verdict was in, it stuck. You didn't appeal the ruling because, as a child, you didn't even know you could. Hell, you didn't even know there was a trial happening

The reason these beliefs have such a strong grip on you today is simple: no one ever questioned them. You didn't have the tools to ask, "*what if this isn't about me?*" In the example above, the child couldn't see that their dad left because he was struggling, not because they weren't lovable. They couldn't recognize that their mom's exhaustion had nothing to do with their worth. They couldn't understand that their teacher's harsh tone was more about the bad day they were having and not their value.

Children don't think that way. They're self-centered by design. It's a survival mechanism. They interpret everything through the lens of, *what does this mean about me?* And so did you.

That's where the trouble begins. These early interpretations—these snap judgments handed down by your inner child—weren't based on reality. They were based on fear, misunderstanding, and incomplete information. But because no one stepped in to cross-examine those beliefs, they became part of your operating system. They became your story.

Fast-forward to adulthood, and those childhood rulings are still running in the background, influencing your decisions, your relationships, and your self-worth.

- In business: You find yourself overworking, terrified that one mistake could make it all come crashing down. That's the voice of the child who believed, *I have to be perfect to be safe.*
- In relationships: You pull away the moment someone gets too close, convinced they'll leave you eventually. That's the child inside, still carrying the belief, *if I let them in, they'll hurt me.*
- In your self-image: You achieve goal after goal, but it never feels like enough. That's the echo of the child who decided, *I have to prove I'm valuable.*

Again, these beliefs don't announce themselves. They operate quietly, like background music you've stopped noticing. But they are there—shaping your actions, your reactions, and even your identity.

Here's the part no one tells you: that eight-year-old is still in charge. They're calling the shots, making decisions, and determining how much love, success, and joy you allow yourself to experience.

Think about it, would you let a child run your business? Negotiate a high-stakes deal? Decide how you show up in your most important relationships? Of course not. But when you let these unchallenged childhood beliefs guide your life, that's exactly what's happening.

The good news? You don't have to keep living this way. You don't have to let an eight-year-old hold the reins.

Take a moment to reflect:

- What's one belief about yourself that feels like an unshakable truth?
- If you trace it back, can you find its roots in childhood?
- What if that belief isn't the whole story? What else could it mean?

These questions aren't about blaming your parents, teachers, or anyone else. They're about giving yourself a fair trial for the first time. They're about recognizing that the child who made those rulings was doing the best they could—but they didn't have the full picture.

And now? You do.

Why It Feels Like Nothing Is Ever Enough

Let me ask you something, how many times have you hit a milestone, celebrated for a moment, and then thought, *okay, what's next?* How many times have you accomplished something incredible—something others would dream of—and felt an uncomfortable emptiness creep in not long after?

If you're being honest, it's probably happened more times than you can count. That feeling—the restlessness, the letdown, the itch to keep moving—isn't a coincidence. It's not just "how you're wired," either. It's a pattern. A pattern driven by something much deeper than ambition or drive.

Hear me when I say, *external achievements can never fill an internal void.*

Let that sink in. You've been running, striving, pushing yourself to the limits, believing that the next win, the next accolade, the next deal will finally give you the peace you're craving. But it hasn't, has it? And it won't. Not because you're broken, but because peace doesn't come from anything outside of you.

The Temporary High of Success

Think back to your last big win—the one you thought would change everything. Maybe it was landing the deal of a lifetime, reaching a financial goal, or standing on stage accepting an award. For a moment, it felt amazing. You were on top of the world. But how long did it last? A few hours? A couple of days? Maybe a week? Then, almost without warning, that familiar ache crept back in.

I know that ache well because I've lived it. Let me share something personal with you.

A few years ago, I hit a milestone I'd spent over a decade chasing: making six figures. For years, that number symbolized everything I thought success would feel like—freedom, fulfillment, confidence. I thought the moment I hit it, everything would finally click.

And when I finally got there—when I moved into my dream neighborhood, started driving my dream car, and reached the life I'd been picturing since I was broke and sleeping in the back of a hookah lounge—do you know what I felt? *Nothing.*

Sure, I celebrated on the surface. I went on vacation. I checked all the boxes of "success." But deep down, I felt empty. Instead of joy, I felt this relentless pressure to keep going. To hit $200K. Then $400K. Then a million.

What I didn't realize at the time was that I wasn't chasing money. I was chasing something much deeper—something I couldn't even name at first.

It wasn't until I sat down with a trusted friend and worked through an exercise to uncover my values that the truth hit me like a brick. Your values are the feelings you're ultimately after—the emotional states that drive your decisions, often buried deep in your subconscious.

The Power of Values

Your values are like the North Star of your life. They guide your decisions, your goals, and even the emotions you prioritize. When you feel fulfilled, it's because you're living in alignment with your values. When you feel restless or empty, it's often because your actions conflict with them.

Many of us aren't even aware of our true values. The values driving our decisions today were often formed in childhood, shaped by the stories we inherited or the experiences we survived.

When I elicited my values, I discovered that my number one value wasn't peace, fulfillment, or joy—it was fame. FAME.

I'd spent my entire adult life chasing external validation, believing that if I could get enough people to admire me, I'd finally feel like I mattered.

Even as I was building the life I'd dreamed of—living in my dream neighborhood, driving my dream car, taking luxury vacations—it never felt like *my* life. It felt like I was performing for an audience I couldn't even see, trying to prove something I couldn't name. And that relentless drive? It wasn't about the money, the milestones, or the applause. It was about me. It was about proving to *myself* that I was enough.

Discovering that fame was my driving value wasn't an easy pill to swallow. I hated that this was buried in my subconscious programming, dictating so much of my life without my awareness. But that moment of clarity was the first step in taking back control—recognizing that I'd been chasing an external validation that could never fill the internal void.

The Real Reason You're Striving

This isn't about ambition. Ambition is healthy. It's about the **need** to achieve—the relentless drive to prove your worth to yourself and the world. That need doesn't come from the adult you sitting here today. It comes from the child inside of you who decided, somewhere along the way, that love, safety, and acceptance had to be earned.

Maybe that belief looked like this:

- If I do well in school, I'll make my parents proud.
- If I achieve more, I'll finally be enough.
- If I work hard, they won't leave me.

Those aren't conscious thoughts anymore. But they've been running in the background, quietly shaping your choices, your goals, and your identity.

For me, it all started in childhood. I moved constantly, attending 14 different schools. Every year, I was the new kid. I went from an all-Black neighborhood to a mostly white one, then to a mostly Latino community. Sometimes I moved from California to the South, and every time, I felt like an outcast. I was always the kid who didn't fit in, always having to reintroduce myself to people who didn't know or respect me.

I was picked on, made fun of, and felt invisible. Somewhere along the way, I must've decided: *If I become famous, I'll never have to introduce myself again. People will already know who I am. They'll respect me. I'll finally belong.*

That realization struck me hard when I looked back. It wasn't just a fleeting thought—it became the silent force driving me for decades. And I remember the exact moment I created the version of myself the world came to know as "Steve Bacon." I was 14 years old, on a bus trip from Georgia to California. I'd had enough. I decided that for my last two years of high school, I was no longer going to be bullied or feel invisible.

I told myself, *If I have to wear a mask to be accepted, then so be it.* And I did. I reinvented myself. I became the bully, the popular guy, the one people couldn't ignore. And for a while, it worked. I finally felt like I belonged. But that wasn't the whole truth. Fame was never the destination—it was a mask. A way to avoid feeling small, invisible, and unworthy. So, as I got older and started achieving milestone after milestone, I realized something: the mask I'd put on wasn't me. It was fake, and it was heavy. It was costing me more than I ever imagined.

The real breakthrough came when I made the choice to take the mask off.

The Fear Beneath the Drive

Here's the thing no one talks about, beneath all that striving is fear. Fear that if you stop running, you'll have to face what's really going on inside. Fear that if you're not achieving, you'll lose your value. Fear that if you're not busy, the emptiness will consume you.

This is why stillness feels so uncomfortable. Why it's easier to keep moving, setting new goals and taking on new challenges, than to sit quietly with yourself. Because deep down, you're afraid of what you might find if you stop.

You want to know the truth about that fear? It's a lie. A story your inner child wrote to keep you safe back then, but it's no longer serving you now. You don't need to prove your worth. You never did. You were enough before you achieved anything, and you'll still be enough if you never achieve another thing.

To break free from this cycle, you first have to see it for what it is. It's not ambition. It's not drive. It's a survival strategy. One that served you well in the past but is now keeping you trapped.

The only way out is to stop chasing external validation and start looking within.

This doesn't mean giving up your goals or ambitions. It means changing the *why* behind them. Instead of striving to prove your worth, what if you pursued your dreams simply because they bring you joy? Instead of working yourself to exhaustion, what if you allowed yourself to rest, knowing that your value isn't tied to your productivity?

Take a moment to reflect on this:

- When was the last time you achieved something and still felt empty afterward?
- What are you afraid might happen if you stop striving for a moment?
- What would it feel like to know, deep down, that you're already enough?

You don't have to have all the answers right now. But recognizing the cycle is the first step. The peace you're looking for isn't out there. It's within you, waiting for you to stop running and finally come home.

Why Peace Feels Out of Reach

Have you ever felt like peace was just around the corner? Like if you could just hit the next milestone—close the deal, meet the right person, or finally balance everything perfectly—it would all click? Maybe you've even had moments where you thought you were almost there. But then the feeling faded, and you were back in the same restless place, wondering, *why does it feel so out of reach?*

Let's pause for a second. What if peace wasn't something you could chase? What if it couldn't be found in working harder, planning better, or achieving more? Maybe, just maybe, peace was never about doing—it was about being.

But being? For someone like you, that might feel like an unfamiliar language. High achievers thrive in motion—solving, building, creating. The idea of slowing down, of just being, can feel unsettling. Like trying to sit still in the middle of a race.

The Disconnect Between Your Success and Your Soul

I know this feeling well. After I'd built the life I thought would bring me peace—the financial success, the dream car, the beautiful home—I found myself asking the same question you might be asking now, *"Why doesn't it feel like enough?"*

That question haunted me until I realized something fundamental. I'd been chasing peace in all the wrong places. I believed that if I just kept pushing harder, I'd finally be able to rest. But peace doesn't work that way.

Here's what I discovered: peace isn't something you can achieve. It's something you have to allow.

And the hardest part? Allowing peace means letting go of the version of yourself that thrives on the chase. The version of you that's always in motion, always solving, always proving. It means stepping away from the hustle and looking inward.

For me, this realization didn't come easy. It came after years of feeling like I was running on a treadmill, chasing something I could never catch. I thought peace was something I had to earn—something that only came after the applause, the milestones, the validation. But no matter how much I achieved, peace felt just out of reach. The truth is, I was looking everywhere except the one place it's always been: within.

The Cost of Chasing Peace

The trap that no one tells you about is chasing peace only makes it more difficult to catch. You hit a goal and feel good for a moment, but before long, the restlessness creeps back in. So, you set another goal, thinking, *"This time it'll be different."* But no matter how much you accomplish, the cycle repeats.

Sound familiar? That's because chasing peace is like chasing the horizon. You can run forever, but you'll never catch it.

I remember the exact moment this hit me. I was standing in the middle of my dream home, staring at the beautiful life I'd built. From the outside, it looked perfect. But inside, I felt completely disconnected. The stillness in that moment was deafening. It forced me to confront the truth I'd been avoiding. Peace wasn't out there. It was in here. But I'd been too afraid to sit still long enough to feel it.

Why Stopping Feels So Hard

Let's be real—stopping isn't easy, is it? Especially when so much of your identity is tied to the constant momentum. The success you've built, the respect you've earned, the admiration of others—it all feels wrapped up in this idea of doing, achieving, and striving.

And then there's the fear. The fear that if you stop, the stillness will overwhelm you. The fear that if you're not chasing, you'll lose your edge. Or worse—that without the chase, you won't know who you are.

I used to feel that way, too. I thought if I stopped moving, if I let go of the hustle, everything I'd built would fall apart. But the truth is, the stillness you're afraid of isn't your enemy. It's your invitation. It's the doorway to something deeper.

What if peace isn't something you have to search for or earn? What if it's something you've had all along, just waiting beneath the noise and motion?

What if the thing you've been running from—stillness—isn't a threat, but a doorway?

Stillness doesn't mean giving up. It doesn't mean you stop building, or creating. It just means you stop looking outside yourself for something that can only be found within. It means listening for that quiet voice that's always been there, steady and sure, reminding you of who you are.

Because maybe peace isn't something you find. Maybe it's something you remember. A part of you that's always been whole, even when you forgot.

Let's sit with this for a moment:

- When was the last time you paused—not to plan your next move, but to simply be present with yourself?
- What would it feel like to stop chasing for a moment and just listen to what's within you?
- What if the peace you've been searching for wasn't something to earn, but something to uncover?

You don't have to answer these questions right now. Just hold them for a while. Let them linger. Because this is where the real journey begins—not in doing more, but in discovering what's already there.

What if the peace you're seeking isn't about doing more, achieving more, or becoming someone else? What if it's about realizing that you're already whole? You don't need to fix yourself—you never did. The answers you've been chasing aren't out there; they've been within you all along.

The stories you've carried, the patterns you've lived by—they've served their purpose. They got you here. But real freedom comes when you let them go and start living in alignment with who you truly are —not who you had to be to survive back then.

Reflective Questions

Let's pause for a moment to reflect:

- What emotions have been driving you? Success, love, belonging?
- What emotions have you been avoiding? Fear, rejection, shame?

- What would it feel like to stop running and embrace the fullness of who you are?

Awareness is the beginning of freedom. You are not your story. The events of your past may have shaped you, but they don't define you. You can step off the merry-go-round of striving and avoiding, and when you do, you'll see that the peace you've been chasing has always been yours.

In the next chapter, we'll explore the emotions you've been avoiding—the ones that quietly shape your decisions and keep you running. Together, we'll face them with compassion and courage, uncovering the freedom and peace that are already yours.

Chapter 2

What Are You Avoiding?

Let me ask you something—and I need you to be really honest with yourself for a second. What are you running from?

Oh, you think you're not running? Okay, let's try this. Why are you so damn busy all the time? Why does your calendar look like a game of Tetris? Why do you scroll through your phone late at night until your eyes burn, or pour yourself that extra glass of wine, or keep saying yes to things you don't even want to do? What are you so afraid will catch up to you in the quiet?

The truth most people don't want to admit is we're all running from something. Nobody wakes up one day and says, "You know what I want? A life built around avoiding my emotions." But life happens. Somewhere along the way, something hurt so bad that you couldn't face it. So, you did what you had to do to survive—you started running.

And running worked…for a while. But emotions don't just go away because you ignore them. They're like shadows—they follow you everywhere. You can't outrun fear, shame, or sadness. Trust me, I've tried.

What happens when you keep running? You stay busy, you keep achieving, you wear your success like a suit of armor—but deep down, you know it's all a distraction. And distractions don't fix the problem; they just delay the inevitable. Because no matter how fast you run or how high you climb, you're still carrying the same weight inside.

Let's be real. You've got the degrees, the career, the money, maybe even the fancy car and the dream house. And yet, here you are, reading this book, wondering why it still feels like something's missing. You tell yourself it's just stress, or that everyone feels this way, but deep down, you know the truth: You're exhausted. Exhausted from trying to be everything for everyone while avoiding the one thing you can't outrun—yourself.

Here's what I need you to know right now. The peace you're chasing? You already have it. It's always been there. Peace isn't something you need to find or earn—it's your natural state. But as long as you keep running, you'll never feel it. Peace doesn't live in the next accomplishment or the next distraction. It lives in the stillness, the quiet, the space you've been avoiding.

Listen, I'm not here to judge you. I see you. I get you. And I'm not about to let you keep running when I know there's a better way. You don't need more success, more goals, or more distractions. What you need is to stop. Pause. And for once, let yourself feel whatever it is you've been avoiding. Because the peace you're looking for? It's not ahead of you—it's already within you. You've just been too busy running to notice.

The Ways We Avoid

Let's talk about avoidance—because if you're anything like me (or any of my clients), you've probably mastered it without even realizing it. Avoidance is sneaky like that. It doesn't wave a big red flag or introduce itself as "emotional hiding." No, it comes disguised as normal, even admirable behaviors.

You tell yourself you're just busy, just being productive. You scroll your phone late at night, convincing yourself you're decompressing, not dodging the silence. You pour yourself another drink, binge-watch that series, or double down on your workload—all in the name of "relaxation" or "getting ahead." But let's be real: these aren't habits—they're shields.

Sound familiar? Here's the tricky part: some forms of avoidance are so socially acceptable—praised, even—that we don't see them for what they are. You're a workaholic? People call you driven. You obsess over self-improvement? People call you disciplined. But underneath the applause, there's a cost—a quiet ache that never goes away because you're solving the wrong problem.

Take this in for a second. Avoidance isn't about the actions themselves; it's about what those actions are covering up. What's the thing you're so afraid to face? What's the emotion you're so desperate to keep buried?

Avoidance doesn't always look like numbing out with Netflix or drinking your weight in wine. Sometimes, it's quieter, subtler—almost invisible. Let me show you what I mean:

- **Overcommitting:** You pack your schedule so full that there's no time to think about what's really bothering you.
- **Perfectionism:** You throw yourself into the grind, chasing flawless results because anything less feels like failure.
- **People-pleasing:** You say yes to everyone, convincing yourself it's kindness, but deep down, you're just avoiding conflict or rejection.
- **The "I'm fine" facade:** You smile, nod, and carry on like everything's okay because admitting otherwise feels too risky.
- **Constant problem-solving:** You become the "fixer" for everyone else's issues, ignoring your own because helping them keeps you from feeling helpless about yourself.

And then there's the big one: **staying busy.** We've all done it—used our to-do lists as distractions. But the truth you don't want to admit is being busy doesn't mean you're thriving. It just means you're avoiding.

Even the most successful people—maybe especially the most successful people—are guilty of this. They hide behind their degrees, their titles, their bank accounts. They've built their identities around being strong, capable, and untouchable. But let me tell you what I've learned after years of working with high achievers. The stronger the mask, the softer the heart underneath.

You know what I'm talking about, don't you? You project confidence, but behind closed doors, you cry when no one's watching. You pride yourself on being the one people rely on, but deep down, you're lonely as hell. You think you're protecting yourself by building walls, but all you're doing is keeping joy and connection out.

Let's not forget the trendy one: "protecting your peace". You tell yourself you're avoiding negativity because you're all about positive energy. But here's the truth, protecting your vibe can be a fancy way of avoiding your triggers. You think it's about boundaries, but sometimes it's just about not wanting to feel uncomfortable.

True emotional freedom doesn't come from avoiding negativity. It comes from having no triggers in the first place. Imagine that for a second—living a life where nothing and no one can knock you off your peace. That's what's possible when you stop running.

What Are You Really Protecting?

Okay, so now we're getting to the heart of it. You've mastered avoidance, crafted walls, and worn the masks—and for what? What are you really protecting? Because all that energy you're spending running and hiding? It's not about keeping others out. It's about keeping yourself from feeling.

Yeah, I said it. You're not protecting your vibe, your peace, or your productivity—you're protecting yourself from your own emotions. And here's the thing about emotions: they don't knock politely and wait to be invited in. They show up, unannounced, demanding to be felt. And the longer you avoid them, the louder they get.

You think you're strong, don't you? And to be fair, you are. But let's talk about the version of strength you've built. You've convinced yourself that strength means keeping it all together, never breaking, never showing vulnerability. But that's not strength—that's fear in a fancy disguise.

Let me tell you about some of the "strongest" people I've ever met: gang leaders, CEOs, high achievers with reputations to protect. You know what they all have in common? They crumble the moment you ask them to face their feelings.

I've seen gang leaders who'd throw hands without hesitation break down when they're asked to talk about their pain. I've worked with executives who run billion-dollar companies but can't have a real conversation with their spouse. That's not strength—it's avoidance.

Here's the real cost of protecting yourself: you keep everyone out, including yourself. You build walls so high that no one can climb them—not your kids, not your spouse, not even the version of you that just wants to breathe.

And the saddest part? You tell yourself you're doing it to survive, but what you're really doing is shrinking. You're so focused on keeping pain out that you end up keeping peace out, too.

Let me ask you this, and I want you to sit with it: What's the thing you've been so afraid to feel? Is it shame? Anger? Grief? Maybe it's fear—fear of failure, rejection, or being seen for who you really are. Or maybe it's loneliness, that aching truth that you've built a life so busy and so big that no one really knows you.

Whatever it is, it's not going to destroy you. I promise. The emotions you're avoiding? They're not the enemy. They're just messengers. They're trying to tell you something, but you've been so busy running that you haven't stopped to listen.

The ironic thing is that the peace and freedom you've been chasing are waiting for you on the other side of those emotions. You think avoiding your feelings is keeping you safe, when it's actually the very thing keeping you stuck.

What if you stopped running? What if, instead of pushing those emotions down, you let them rise to the surface? What if you faced them with the same courage you bring to the boardroom, the courtroom, or the stage? I can't repeat this enough—the freedom you want doesn't come from running—it comes from facing what you've been running from.

You've been running so long that you've forgotten what stillness feels like. And sure, you might think it's working. You've built the life, the career, the image. But at what cost? Because the truth is, every time you avoid your emotions, you pay a price.

Avoidance might feel like relief in the moment—a quick fix, a distraction, a way to catch your breath. But it's not free. It costs you energy, connection, and most of all, peace. You're borrowing from yourself, taking out emotional loans with sky-high interest rates.

Reality check: avoidance doesn't erase what you're running from. It just pushes it down. But like trying to hold a beach ball underwater, it doesn't stay there. The more you push, the harder it fights to rise. And when it does? It's messy. It spills into your relationships, your decisions, your health—every part of your life.

When you avoid sadness, anger, or fear, you're not just numbing the bad—you're numbing the good, too. Joy, love, connection—they get blocked right along with the pain. You end up living life on mute, never fully feeling anything. Sure, you avoid the lows, but you miss the highs, too.

Ever notice how nothing feels as good as it should? The vacation is nice, but it doesn't touch that ache inside. The promotion feels great—for a minute. The applause fills the room, but not your heart. That's the cost of avoidance. It's like eating a meal without tasting the food. You're consuming life, but you're not savoring it.

Avoidance doesn't just steal your joy—it steals your relationships. You can't connect deeply with others if you're not connected to yourself. The walls you build to keep pain out also keep love out. And let's be honest, the people closest to you feel it. Your kids feel it when you're physically present but emotionally checked out. Your partner feels it when you shut down instead of opening up. Your friends feel it when your "I'm fine" doesn't match the look in your eyes.

And you feel it, too. In the quiet moments, when the distractions fade, and it's just you and the ache you can't outrun. You tell yourself you're strong, that you're holding it all together. But deep down, you know. You know there's a cost, and you're the one paying it.

Here's the part most people miss: avoidance doesn't just affect your personal life—it sabotages your success. How many opportunities have you passed up because of fear? How many conflicts have you avoided that could've led to breakthroughs? How much energy have you wasted managing the emotions you won't face?

Think about it. How much more powerful, more impactful, more present could you be if you weren't dragging this invisible weight behind you? Avoidance might feel like control, but it's actually the opposite. It's a leash holding you back from your full potential.

So, here's the question, and I encourage you to sit with it: What is avoidance costing you? Not just in dollars or time, but in joy, connection, and freedom? What could your life look like if you stopped running? What would it feel like to face the thing you've been avoiding and realize it wasn't as scary as you thought?

Avoidance isn't protection. It's a cage. And the key to freedom isn't running faster—it's stopping, turning around, and facing what you've been running from.

There's another layer to avoidance that we need to address: the ego. Avoidance isn't just about dodging emotions—it's about protecting the identity you've built. The version of you that looks strong, successful, untouchable. And while it might look good on the outside, it's suffocating your peace on the inside.

It reminds me of a parable Jesus told about a rich prince who came to him, asking how to enter the Kingdom of Heaven. The man had everything—wealth, status, power—but still, he felt something was missing. So, Jesus told him, "Sell everything you have."

Now, this wasn't about glorifying poverty or saying that wealth is wrong. Jesus was teaching the man a deeper lesson: *You are everything with nothing.* He wanted the man to see that his worth wasn't tied to his possessions, his status, or the identity he had built. But the prince couldn't let go. His identity was so wrapped up in his stuff that he walked away sad.

That's why Jesus said, "It's easier for a camel to pass through the eye of a needle than for a rich man to enter the Kingdom of Heaven." It wasn't about the money—it was about the ego. The more you build your identity around what you do, what you have, and what others think of you, the harder it becomes to find peace. You can't access heaven—the state of presence—if you're trapped in your ego.

The ego is a master illusionist. It convinces you that your worth is tied to what you achieve, what you own, and how others see you. It whispers, *"If you stop striving, you'll lose everything."* The truth? The ego doesn't protect you—it imprisons you. It builds walls, not to keep you safe, but to keep you small. It tells you that vulnerability is weakness. The more you cling to the identity you've built, the harder it becomes to hear the voice inside whispering, '*You are already enough.*'

The prince in the parable isn't just a character from an old story—it's you. It's me. It's all of us. We build our lives around what we think will bring us peace—status, wealth, success—and we cling to those things like they define us. We tell ourselves, *this is who I am,* and we'll fight tooth and nail to protect that identity.

The ego convinces you that your worth is tied to your achievements, that your peace is somewhere in the future, and that you're not enough as you are. And as long as you believe that, you'll keep running. You'll keep avoiding. You'll keep trying to fix an inside problem with outside solutions.

But what if you could let go of all that? What if you could stop playing the role and just be? What if peace wasn't something you had to chase but something you could return to, simply by stopping the cycle?

The ego will tell you that letting go means losing everything you've built. But the opposite is true. Letting go of the ego isn't about giving up—it's about reclaiming. Reclaiming your freedom. Reclaiming your joy. Reclaiming the life that's waiting for you beneath the noise.

What Would It Feel Like to Stop Running?

Close your eyes for a moment and imagine this: waking up and feeling at peace, not because you've achieved something or proven yourself, but because you're no longer at war with yourself. Picture a life where you're not ruled by your triggers, where you're not projecting your pain onto others, where you're no longer hiding behind your degrees, your bank account, or your influence.

Imagine thriving relationships with your kids, your spouse, and—most importantly—with yourself. A life where you're not lonely in a crowd, not crying behind closed doors, not constantly questioning why you're unhappy when you have everything you thought you wanted.

This isn't a fantasy. It's your natural state. Peace is your birthright. Emotional freedom is your default setting. You don't have to create it—you just have to stop running long enough to see it.

Let's be honest—stopping feels terrifying, doesn't it? You've built a life on motion, on doing, on achieving. Slowing down feels risky, even dangerous. You wonder, "If I stop, will everything fall apart? Will I lose my edge? Will I lose myself?" But the truth is, stopping isn't losing—it's finding. Slowing down doesn't mean giving up your ambition; it means giving it purpose. It means using your drive to build something aligned with who you are, instead of running from who you're not. What if slowing down isn't the end of your success, but the beginning of your freedom?

Every time you avoid your emotions, you're paying a price. Maybe it's a fractured relationship because you avoided vulnerability. Maybe it's your health, strained by stress and bottled-up feelings. Maybe it's the joy you can't fully experience because you've numbed the pain.

Avoidance isn't just costing you—it's costing the people who love you. Your kids see you chasing success, but they don't see you. Your partner feels the distance, even when you're in the same room. The people closest to you are waiting for you to come home—not just physically, but emotionally.

And deep down, you know it. You feel the ache, the emptiness, the nagging sense that something's missing. That's your soul's way of calling you back to yourself. It's not failure—it's an invitation.

The Invitation: Facing What You've Been Avoiding

You've been running long enough. The peace you're chasing? It's not in your next promotion, your next relationship, or your next achievement. It's here. Now. Within you. And it's been waiting for you to stop and turn around.

Facing what you've been avoiding isn't easy. It might feel like the silence is screaming at you, like the emotions you've buried will overwhelm you. But let me tell you from personal experience, they won't break you. In fact, facing them is the only thing that will set you free.

Take a deep breath. This is the moment you've been avoiding, but it's also the moment you've been waiting for. On the other side of this discomfort is everything you've been searching for: peace, freedom, connection, joy.

Reflective Questions

Take a moment to reflect:

- What emotions have you been avoiding?
- What identity are you clinging to that no longer serves you?
- What would it feel like to face your triggers instead of avoiding them?
- What might happen if you stopped running?

You don't have to have all the answers right now. Just start with this. What's one thing you've been running from that you're ready to face today?

Chapter 3

Putting the Game of Life on Hard

Chapters 1 and 2 showed you what you're striving for and what you're avoiding. This chapter is about understanding how you've made both of those things harder than they need to be. It's about seeing how you've set up your life in a way that makes it difficult to feel the emotions you deeply desire—like peace, joy, and success—and way too easy to feel the ones you're running from—like shame, fear, or rejection.

Let's connect the dots. You've identified the feelings you've been chasing, the ones driving your goals, achievements, and ambitions. And you've started to see the emotions you've been avoiding—the ones lurking beneath the surface, steering your decisions in ways you didn't realize. Now, we're going to explore how you've unknowingly put yourself in a position where the game of life feels almost unwinnable.

Before we dive in, let me take a moment to acknowledge something. The last chapter came with a bit of tough love, didn't it? That tone wasn't there to make you feel called out or judged—it was there because I care too much to let you keep running from the truth. Sometimes, the most loving thing I can do is hold up a mirror so you can see what's really going on. But this chapter is about meeting you with that same love, guiding you to see that life doesn't have to feel like an uphill battle. You're not broken; you've just been playing by rules that don't serve you anymore and that's what we're here to change.

It's not just the striving or the avoiding—it's the rules you've set for yourself. Somewhere along the way, you decided that certain emotions, like pride or happiness, are only accessible after jumping through endless hoops. At the same time, you've made it so easy to feel the things you don't want to feel. One critical comment, one perceived failure, or one rejection can send you spiraling.

This isn't a judgment—it's a wake-up call. Because once you recognize this pattern, you can begin to shift it. You can see how the conditions you've set for yourself are not just unfair; they're unnecessary. Life doesn't have to be this hard. The question is: are you ready to rewrite the rules?

The Rules You Didn't Know You Were Following

Have you ever stopped to wonder why life feels so complicated? Why some people seem to walk through life with ease while you feel like you're climbing a never-ending mountain? It's not because they're smarter, luckier, or more deserving. The truth is, they're not playing by the same rules you are—and most importantly, they probably aren't even aware of it.

Every single one of us is living by a set of invisible rules, and most of them were written long before we even knew what life was about. These aren't rules you consciously chose; they were handed to you, piece by piece, during your early years. Back then, you didn't have the tools or the perspective to question them. You just absorbed them, believing they were the way the world worked.

You might not think of yourself as someone who follows "rules," but here's how it looks:

- You tell yourself you can't feel proud unless you've hit a certain milestone.
- You believe that being loved means never making mistakes.
- You've convinced yourself that joy only comes after the struggle.

These beliefs might feel like truths, but they're just rules—rules you didn't create with your adult mind, and most of them don't serve you anymore.

When I sat down with one of my clients, we did an exercise to explore his values—the emotions he was striving to feel and the ones he was working so hard to avoid. He told me he wanted to feel successful, accomplished, and respected. Those were his "move-toward" values. But when we got deeper into it, he realized just how hard he had made it to feel those emotions.

For him to feel successful, he had to accomplish a laundry list of things: make a certain amount of money, earn a specific title, have everyone's approval, and never make a mistake. And even when he managed to check every box, the feeling didn't last. There was always a new goal, a higher bar, a moving finish line.

And then we flipped it. I asked him about his "move-away" values—the emotions he didn't want to feel. Things like shame, failure, and rejection. And here's where it hit him: For him to feel successful, he had to climb Mount Everest, but for him to feel shame? All it took was asking someone for help.

Think about that. He had built his life to make it nearly impossible to feel the emotions he wanted and incredibly easy to feel the ones he didn't. He had unconsciously designed a game he couldn't win.

The same rules that were created to protect you as a child are now the ones holding you back as an adult. But here's the good news: The rules are yours. And that means you have the power to change them.

How Hard Are You Making It to Feel Good?

Let's pause for a second and be honest—how often do you give yourself permission to feel good, to truly let yourself experience joy, pride, or peace? For most people, it's rare, and it's not because life isn't offering those opportunities. It's because you've made it so hard to feel them.

Think about it. What has to happen for you to feel successful? For you to feel loved? For you to feel worthy? If you're like most people, the checklist is endless. You've tied your happiness to external milestones—ones that keep moving the moment you get close.

You tell yourself, "*I'll feel proud of myself when I hit that next income level.*" Or, "*I'll feel happy when my relationship looks a certain way*", or "*when I lose 20 pounds*", or "*when people finally recognize my accomplishments.*" But the bar keeps rising, doesn't it? No matter how much you achieve, it's never quite enough. You've created a system where joy is always just out of reach.

One of my clients, let's call him Paul, was a perfect example of this. When we sat down to uncover his values, he said he wanted to feel accomplished. But when I asked him what needed to happen for him to feel that way, the list was exhausting. He'd built so many hoops to jump through, it's no wonder he felt burned out and unfulfilled.

Then I asked him a simple question, "What would happen if you decided you were already accomplished? Right now. Without needing to do or prove anything else?"

That's when it hit him. He realized he'd been living by someone else's definition of accomplished—one he'd picked up from childhood, from society, from people who had nothing to do with his current life. And yet, he was letting those rules dictate his emotions, his decisions, and his peace of mind. When we broke it down, he saw how much easier he made it to feel like a failure than to feel accomplished.

For Paul, one harsh comment from a colleague could leave him spiraling into self-doubt. One missed goal could make him feel unworthy. And yet, for him to feel accomplished? He needed to move mountains.

What about you? Have you ever stopped to ask yourself, "Why have I made it so hard to feel good? And whose rules am I even following?"

Feeling joy, peace, or pride doesn't have to be complicated. You don't need to wait for some external milestone to arrive. The only person who gets to decide what success, love, or worthiness means for you is you. And you have the power to choose to feel those things now—not someday when the stars align, but right here, right now.

How Easy Are You Making It to Feel Bad?

Now let's flip the script. If you've made it nearly impossible to feel good, how easy have you made it to feel bad? Be honest—how little does it take to spiral into self-doubt or feel unworthy? One mistake? A single comment from someone? A glance that didn't feel quite right?

It's wild when you think about it. The same person who needs a perfect performance to feel accomplished can feel like a failure after one small misstep. The same person who ties their worth to a long checklist can feel worthless from a single criticism.

This isn't a coincidence; it's how we're wired. Your brain has a survival mechanism that's always on high alert, scanning for threats. And while this might have been helpful when we were trying to avoid predators, it's not so great when the "threat" is a coworker's offhand remark or a perceived insult from your spouse.

Take one of my clients, Rachel. She was a powerhouse—running a successful company, raising three kids, and juggling more than most people could imagine. But when we started digging into her patterns, it became clear how easy she made it for herself to feel bad.

One example in particular stood out. Rachel hated feeling like she wasn't doing enough as a mom. All it took was one rushed evening where she couldn't make dinner or help with homework for her to feel like a failure. Never mind that she was managing an entire company, providing for her family, and being a constant source of love for her kids. That one moment was enough to trigger a landslide of guilt.

And then there was her definition of success at work. Rachel could have 10 meetings go perfectly, but if the 11th didn't go as planned, she'd fixate on it for days. One piece of constructive feedback could cancel out weeks of wins in her mind.

Sound familiar? Most of us have conditioned ourselves to see mistakes, rejections, and setbacks as signs of failure. And because we've made it so easy to feel bad, the emotional toll is heavy. It's exhausting to live in a world where the tiniest crack feels like the foundation is crumbling.

Why Does This Happen?

The truth is, your brain learned this pattern long ago. As a child, feeling unworthy or rejected could feel life-threatening. If you disappointed a parent, got scolded by a teacher, or felt invisible at home, your young mind processed those moments as dangerous. To avoid those feelings, you developed hyper-awareness—always scanning for signs you might mess up, upset someone, or fall short.

Fast forward to adulthood, and those same patterns are running your life. Your brain is still wired to overemphasize negativity and dismiss the positive. It's why one critical comment can feel louder than a hundred compliments. It's why one missed goal can overshadow every milestone you've achieved.

However, those rules aren't protecting you anymore. They're holding you hostage.

What if you decided to make it harder to feel bad? What if you questioned the stories that tell you a single mistake erases your worth? What if you gave yourself the grace to mess up, to be human, to let things go?

You can rewrite the rules. The power isn't in the external events—it's in how you interpret them. And right now, you're the one holding the pen.

The Wake-Up Call: Why Are You Really Chasing This?

One day, whether you like it or not, you're going to get a front-row seat to your own mortality. Maybe it'll come in a quiet moment of reflection, or maybe it'll hit you like a freight train, but at some point, you'll have to face the question, *what was it all for?*

Was it for the titles, the money, the applause? Or was it for the moments you didn't even realize were happening—the laughs, the hugs, the quiet sunsets you were too busy to notice?

Look, I'm not saying ambition is bad. Ambition is what makes life exciting, what keeps us moving forward. But when ambition becomes the master instead of the servant, when it's driven by the need to prove your worth rather than express it, that's when you lose sight of what really matters.

Do you even know *why* you want what you want? Or are you just following a script someone else handed you?

How much of your life has been spent chasing the dream that was sold to you? The house, the car, the income—was it *your* dream, or was it marketing?

Here's a truth that'll slap you awake if you let it. The world doesn't care about your happiness. It cares about your consumption. It cares about keeping you striving, buying, achieving—because that's how it survives. But you? You're not here to just survive. You're here to *live*.

The Stories of Regret

I used to sit down with seniors and ask them about life. People in their fourth quarter, who've lived the games we're playing now. And do you know what they said? It wasn't, *"I wish I'd made more money,"* or, *"I wish I'd worked more hours."*

It was things like:

"I wish I'd spent more time with my family."

"I wish I hadn't cared so much about what people thought of me."

"I wish I'd let myself be happier."

They'd tell me how they were so focused on getting to the next goal that they forgot to enjoy the ride. And when they finally arrived? The high lasted five minutes before the emptiness set in. They'd look back and realize the journey was the point all along.

It's remarkable what the elders figure out, isn't it? After decades of striving, building, achieving, and chasing dreams, they come to the same realization: none of it ever mattered as much as they thought it did. The accolades, the milestones, the external markers of success—they were distractions from what was truly important: the relationships they built, the love they gave, and the peace they found within themselves.

How many more stories, movies, or interviews do you need to hear before it clicks for you? How many more cautionary tales of people climbing to the top only to realize the mountain was empty? What if you borrowed wisdom from your future self today and rewrote your rules now? Imagine the quality of life you could create if you didn't have to wait until the fourth quarter of life to figure it out. And if we're keeping it all the way 100, that's assuming you'll make it to the fourth quarter. I know that's tough to hear, but you and I both know it's true.

What if you chose to make peace and emotional freedom your priority *now*?

This isn't about giving up ambition. It's about questioning why you want what you want and whether the rules you've set are serving you—or making your life harder. Are you really striving for what matters to you, or have you bought into someone else's version of success? Borrowing from the wisdom of those who've walked the road before you, you can choose to make it easy to feel fulfilled and stop putting the game of life on hard.

Imagine you're on a bus, traveling from one coast to the other. Let's say you've always dreamed of arriving at your destination—it's been your life's goal. But instead of enjoying the ride, you take a sleeping pill. You skip the views, the conversations, the stops along the way—all because you just want to get there.

Then you arrive, and it's… fine. Not bad, but not what you imagined. And someone asks, *"Well, at least the ride was beautiful, wasn't it?"* And that's when it hits you: You missed the whole point. The beauty was in the journey, and you were too busy rushing to see it.

Life is like that bus ride. You don't get a do-over. This is your one-way trip. Are you awake for it?

Your ego doesn't want you to hear this. It's addicted to the chase. It feeds on the next goal, the next accomplishment, the next validation. And as long as you're striving for the next hit, you'll never experience the peace that's already here.

Your ego wants you to believe that peace is something you have to earn. The truth is, the world doesn't care about your rules. It doesn't care how many degrees you've earned, how many awards you've collected, or how much wealth you've amassed. The world will keep moving forward, indifferent to your achievements. And that's not a bad thing—it's actually freeing.

This is what it means to be in the world but not of it. When you build your life around external validation, you tether your worth to a world that isn't designed to fulfill you. But when you untether, when you decide that your value comes from within and not from what you do or how others perceive you, you stop making the game harder than it has to be.

Being in the world but not of it means defining success on your own terms. It's choosing to live by your own rules—not society's, not your family's, not the ones you wrote as a scared child trying to survive. It's recognizing that peace and freedom are already available to you, but you have to stop chasing the world's approval to access them. The irony is, when you do this, you actually show up in the world with more power, more love, and more clarity. Because now, you're playing by your own rules.

Peace is your natural state. The only thing keeping you from it is the idea that you have to keep running to find it.

So, let me ask you. What are you chasing, and why?

Is it truly what you want, or is it what you think you're supposed to want? Have you bought into the world's idea of success, or have you taken the time to define your own? Because if you're not clear on that, you'll spend your whole life running someone else's race.

And at the end of the day, here's what I know for sure: There's nothing wrong with wanting to succeed. But if you're not awake for the journey—if you're not present for the moments that matter—then no amount of success will ever feel like enough.

Living Life on Easy Mode

Let's pause for a moment and imagine what life could look like if you flipped the rules. What if you made it easy to feel joy, peace, and pride—and harder to feel unworthy or ashamed? What if you gave yourself permission to experience happiness without attaching it to conditions or achievements?

Living life on easy mode doesn't mean you stop caring about success or striving for more. It means redefining the game so it works in your favor. It means making decisions from a place of worthiness, not proving it. Here's what living life on easy mode looks like:

- Giving yourself permission to feel good, just because you're alive.
- No longer tying your worth to your achievements or mistakes.
- Being kind to yourself when things don't go as planned.
- Allowing yourself to be seen, flaws and all, without fear of rejection.

This is what it means to rewrite your story. It's not about abandoning ambition; it's about stepping off the treadmill of "never enough" and allowing yourself to savor the moments that matter. It's about letting go of the old rules and creating a new way of being—one driven by love, joy, and self-compassion, not fear or shame.

The good news? You've already taken the first step by becoming aware of the game you've been playing. The next step is to start questioning the rules you've been living by—and then rewriting them to match the truth of who you are.

Peace isn't something you earn after years of striving. It's your natural state. It's already here, waiting for you to stop running, stop proving, and just be.

As we move into the next chapter, we'll dig deeper into who you *think* you are—and more importantly, who you *really* are. Because rewriting the rules begins with understanding the stories you've been living by and the identity you've built around them.

Reflective Questions

Let's take a moment to reflect:

- What is it that you truly want?
- Why do you want it? Is it for you, or for someone else's approval?
- Are you enjoying the ride, or are you just trying to get to the destination?
- What have you been making it hard to feel?
- What have you been making it too easy to feel?
- What's one area of your life where you've made it easy to feel bad?

- What emotions are you striving to feel, and what conditions have you tied to those feelings?
- What's one emotion you could choose to feel today, without waiting for external validation?
- What would happen if you let yourself feel good even when things aren't perfect?
- How can you start questioning the rules that lead to that pattern?
- What story have you been living by—and what else could it mean?

You don't have to have all the answers right now. But don't wait until you're in the fourth quarter to start asking these questions. Because the life you're chasing is happening right now. Are you awake enough to see it?

This isn't about fixing yourself—**you are not broken**. It's about seeing yourself clearly, letting go of the old rules, and choosing to live differently.

Chapter 4

You Are Not Who You Think You Are

Picture this: One day, as a kid, you found a pair of glasses lying around. No one handed them to you—you just picked them up. At first, they were kind of cool. They helped you make sense of the world, showed you where you fit in, and protected you from the things that felt overwhelming. So, you kept wearing them.

The twist? Those glasses weren't exactly clear. Over time, the lenses got scratched, smudged, and warped. Each experience—every rejection, every criticism, every painful moment—left its mark. And without even realizing it, you began seeing life through those distorted lenses. You thought they were helping, but they were actually changing how you saw everything, including yourself.

Now, imagine you've been wearing those same glasses for so long, you've forgotten they're even there. You walk through life seeing yourself as small, not because you are, but because the lenses have a crack right in the middle. You see others as critical, not because they are, but because the tint on the lenses is darkened by old wounds. And you see success as just out of reach—not because it is, but because the edges of the lenses are smudged with doubt.

Those glasses were never meant to stay on forever. They were useful when you first picked them up, but now they're holding you back. You're bumping into walls, misreading situations, and questioning your own worth, all because you forgot you're wearing them.

What if you could take them off? What if, for the first time, you could see yourself and the world as they really are—clear, bright, and free of distortion?

That's what we're here to do in this book: help you take off the glasses, clean the lenses, or maybe even ditch them entirely. Because who you *think* you are right now isn't the real you—it's just what those glasses have shown you. And trust me, the view without them? It's a game-changer.

How Self-Image Controls Performance

When I was in my early 20s, I went to a networking event in one of the wealthiest neighborhoods in California. At the time, I didn't have much money, but I did have a black suit—my only suit. It wasn't anything fancy, just something I'd found on clearance. Over time, I'd ironed it so many times it had started to shine (I didn't know you weren't supposed to iron suits back then).

Walking into that event, I felt out of place immediately. My mind started racing: *These people think I don't belong here. They can tell I don't have money. They see I'm Black—they probably don't trust me.* My heart was pounding, my palms were sweating, and I felt this overwhelming need to either prove myself or leave.

No one said a single word to me. No one even looked at me funny. Every negative thought I had about how others were judging me wasn't coming from them—it was coming from me.

I stood there for 20 minutes, locked in a mental war with myself, until I finally left. On the drive home, I blamed the people at the event. *They're racist. They're judgmental. They didn't make me feel welcome.* But looking back, I now know that wasn't true.

Years later, when I was working with Bob Proctor, he said something that hit me like a ton of bricks: "Self-image isn't what other people think of you. It's what you think other people think of you."

In that moment, everything clicked. No one at that event judged me. The only person judging me was me. I had walked into that room wearing glasses tinted by years of insecurity and self-doubt, and I blamed the people around me for the way I felt. Sound familiar?

Here's the thing about self-image: It's not reality. It's a story you carry with you, and it filters everything you see, hear, and experience. You don't respond to what's happening—you respond to what you *think* is happening.

That's why someone can tell you they love you, and you don't believe them. Or why someone can compliment your work, and you dismiss it as pity. It's all filtered through your self-image, and if your self-image says you're not enough, no amount of validation will feel real.

As I walked out of that networking event years ago, still caught up in my feelings of not belonging, I couldn't see the truth: none of those people were judging me. It wasn't their voices in my head—it was mine. The belief that "I don't belong here" wasn't a fact; it was a story I had written long before I even put on that shiny suit.

This is what I want you to understand. Your self-image isn't some random collection of thoughts. It's a belief system—a cycle that starts with the meaning you assigned to an event as a child. That belief shapes how you think, which drives how you feel, which dictates what you do, and ultimately determines the results you get.

The Self-Fulfilling Prophecy

To show you how this plays out, let me take you back to a belief that ran my life for years—one that I didn't even realize was driving me until much later.

When I was eight years old, I created a story: **"The women who love me will leave me."**

It started the day my mom dropped me off at my grandmother's house, as she'd done many times before. Except this time, she didn't come back. Instead, a man I only met once before showed up, claiming to be my dad, saying I was going to live with him now. And to drive it home, he told me, "Your mom doesn't want you anymore."

In that moment, my eight-year-old mind made sense of what was happening the only way it could: *If a woman loves me, she'll eventually leave me.*

I didn't know it at the time, but that belief became the lens through which I saw every relationship moving forward. And as a kid, my brain—trying to protect me from ever feeling that kind of pain again—turned that belief into a strategy. I decided: **Never trust a woman when she says she loves you, because she'll leave.**

Fast forward to my first marriage, and that belief wasn't just a thought in the back of my mind. It was the invisible script running the show. Every time my wife told me she loved me, I didn't feel joy or comfort. My mind went straight to suspicion. I'd think, *"She's lying. She's going to leave. And if she's going to leave, she'll probably cheat first."*

Every man she interacted with became a potential threat. If she came home a little late, my mind would spiral, *"She's probably cheating on me."* Those thoughts triggered emotions—fear, jealousy, rage—and those emotions drove my actions. I started questioning her every move. I became controlling, accusatory, and, eventually, abusive. I lashed out in anger, trying to control the situation.

And the result? She left. My behavior pushed her away.

When she did, my belief system whispered, *"See? I told you. The women who love you will leave you."*

The same belief that I created as a child, the same belief I thought was protecting me, ended up creating the very thing I was most afraid of. I was living out a self-fulfilling prophecy, playing the victim to my own creation.

I didn't have the emotional tools as a kid to process what was happening, so my mind did the only thing it could: It created a story. And that story became my belief.

It's wild, isn't it? The very thing I was trying to avoid—being left—was the result of my own actions. I created the outcome I feared most, but because of the belief I was living by, I couldn't see it. Instead, I was reinforcing the cycle over and over again.

This is what a self-fulfilling prophecy looks like. It's the reason people say, "Why does this always happen to me?" The answer is almost always the same. Your beliefs are shaping your reality, even when you don't realize it.

Here's the part that's hardest to accept but most liberating to understand. You're not just the victim in these stories—you're the creator. And while that might feel heavy at first, it's actually the most empowering truth you'll ever learn. Because if you're the creator of the cycle, you can change it.

Are you playing the victim to your own creations?

It's easy to look at the results in your life and blame the external world—your circumstances, the people around you, the hand you were dealt. But much of what you're experiencing today is a direct reflection of the beliefs you've carried for years.

The beliefs you created as a kid—when you didn't know any better—are still calling the shots. And if those beliefs are based on any kind of fear, shame, or unworthiness, they're likely creating the very outcomes you're trying so hard to avoid.

The good news is that just like you created those beliefs, you can unlearn them. You can rewrite the story.

The Belief Theory Framework

Beliefs are like the architects of your life, quietly shaping everything from your thoughts to your results. They're invisible, but their impact is everywhere—guiding your choices, dictating your emotions, and even influencing how you see yourself. Most of these beliefs were formed when you were too young to even understand what was happening.

Let's break it down.

Picture a cycle. At the start is a belief. That belief generates your thoughts, which then influences your emotions. Your emotions drive your actions, and your actions create results. But here's where it gets tricky: Those results feed right back into the original belief, reinforcing it over and over again.

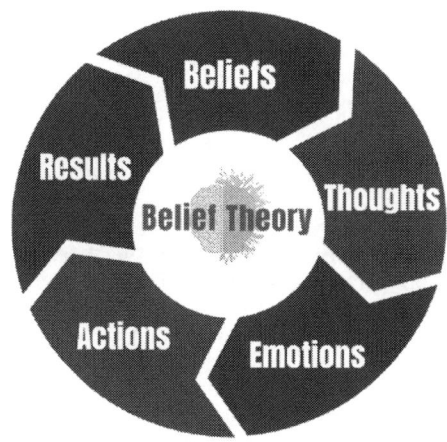

This is how it works for all of us:

1. **Beliefs** form in childhood as we try to make sense of the world.
2. Those beliefs generate **thoughts** about ourselves and others.
3. Those thoughts create **emotions**, which influence how we feel and react.
4. Those emotions drive our **actions**—the decisions we make and the behaviors we repeat.
5. And those actions create **results** that reinforce the original belief.

It's a loop—a cycle that keeps you trapped in the same patterns over and over again. And until you challenge the belief at its root, the cycle continues.

Now, let's connect this back to self-image. Every cycle—every belief that creates thoughts, emotions, actions, and results—feeds into how you see yourself. Over time, these repeated experiences create your self-image.

If your beliefs tell you that you're unworthy, incapable, or unlovable, your self-image will reflect that. You'll act in ways that reinforce those beliefs, and the results will confirm what you've believed all along. It's like adding layer after layer of distorted paint to a canvas until the original picture is almost unrecognizable.

But let me tell you, the canvas underneath is still whole. Your self-image might be built on layers of old beliefs, but those beliefs aren't you. They're just stories you've been living by. And the moment you start questioning them, they begin falling apart.

What beliefs might be running your life right now?

Think about the areas where you feel stuck, unfulfilled, or constantly striving without satisfaction. Behind every struggle is a belief. Maybe it's something like:

- *I'm only worthy if I'm perfect.*
- *Success requires struggle.*
- *People will hurt me if I let them get too close.*

Whatever the belief is, it's creating a cycle. And that cycle is shaping your self-image, keeping you trapped in patterns that don't serve you.

However, beliefs aren't facts. They're just stories you've been telling yourself, and you have the power to rewrite them. But first, you have to see them for what they are.

The Belief Theory Framework is like a map, showing you how your inner world shapes your outer reality. It's not about blame—it's about awareness. Because once you see the cycle, you can step outside of it. You can challenge the beliefs that no longer serve you, change the thoughts that hold you back, and create a new self-image that aligns with the life you want to live.

The next time you find yourself saying, "Why does this always happen to me?" pause. Look for the belief at the start of the cycle. Ask yourself, *Is this true? Is this serving me?* Because the moment you start questioning your beliefs, you take the first step toward breaking the cycle—and that's where real freedom begins.

The Picasso of Self-Image

Let's break this down, layer by layer, using the framework in the diagram. Your self-image—how you see yourself through the eyes of others—is like a Picasso painting. From a distance, it looks like a complete picture, but when you step closer, you see the fragmented, distorted shapes. It's a patchwork of childhood experiences, decisions, beliefs, and a vague sense of identity that all seem to fit together—but don't really align.

Here's how it happens:

1. **Childhood Experiences**
   When you were a kid, everything that happened around you left an impression. But here's the catch, you didn't have the tools nor life experience to interpret those experiences accurately. You saw the world in black and white, thinking everything was about you *and only one side of the situation.* These misinterpretations became the foundation of your reality.
2. **Decisions**
   From those misinterpreted experiences, you made decisions—quick ones, emotional ones. You decided how to protect yourself, who you needed to be, and what you had to avoid. These decisions were your way of surviving, but they were made with the emotional logic of a child.
3. **Beliefs**
   Over time, those decisions solidified into beliefs. Beliefs are like the scaffolding of your self-image, the structure holding up the picture. More importantly, beliefs don't have to be true to feel real.
4. **Picture (Vague and Distorted)**
   All those beliefs form a picture of who you think you are. But it's

vague and incomplete because it's based on fragmented pieces of your past, not the truth of who you really are. It's like trying to put together a puzzle with the wrong pieces. You end up with a picture, but it doesn't make sense.
5. **Self-Image**
   This distorted picture is what you carry into adulthood, believing it's who you are. It shapes how you show up in relationships, at work, and in every decision you make. But here's the problem: it's not the real you. It's a reflection of old stories, outdated beliefs, and decisions you made when you didn't have the full picture.

Why does this matter?

The Picasso painting isn't the truth—it's just what you've been looking at. But because it's all you've known, it feels real. As long as you live by this distorted picture, you'll never see yourself clearly. You'll keep operating from old beliefs, making decisions that reinforce those beliefs, and wondering why nothing changes.

But what if you could step back? What if you could challenge the experiences, decisions, and beliefs that formed this picture? What if you could start painting a new one—one that's whole, clear, and aligned with the truth of who you really are?

This is your invitation to take a step back and question everything. Because the truth is, you're not the fragmented painting you see—you're the artist holding the brush. And it's time to start painting something new.

The Power of Awareness

Think about where we started. In Chapter 1, we uncovered what you're striving for—the feelings you've been chasing through success, validation, and external achievements. Then, in Chapter 2, we turned the spotlight on what you're avoiding—the emotions that feel too heavy to face, the ones you've been running from. And in Chapter 3, we revealed how you've set up the game of life on hard mode—making it nearly impossible to feel the emotions you want while making it way too easy to feel the ones you don't.

Now, here in Chapter 4, we're zooming in on the *why*. Why does life feel like this endless cycle of striving and avoiding? It all comes down to your self-image—the invisible story driving your every thought, emotion, and action. Now that you see the story for what it is, you've taken the first step toward freedom.

Awareness is where it begins. You can't change what you can't see. But now you see it. You see how your childhood experiences shaped decisions, which created beliefs, which painted a distorted picture of who you think you are. And for the first time, you're realizing that the story isn't the truth. The glasses don't define you. The story doesn't define you. It's just a story. And stories can be rewritten.

Choice and Responsibility

You've been striving for feelings like peace, joy, and success while running from feelings like rejection, shame, or fear. But why are those feelings so hard to grasp? Why do the same patterns keep repeating? It's because the story you've been living by—your self-image—has made them hard to access. And until you challenge that story, you'll stay stuck in the same loop.

But now, with this awareness, you have a choice. Will you keep playing by the old rules, or will you create a new game? Will you keep letting your self-image—the patchwork of childhood meanings—run your life, or will you step into the truth of who you really are?

This isn't about blaming yourself for the past. You didn't choose those beliefs as a child—you picked them up to survive. But now, as an adult, you can choose to put them down. The moment you realize the glasses are just tools—ones you can remove—you reclaim your power.

Awareness alone won't rewrite the story. It's the first step, but it's not the last. Recognizing the story is one thing. Deciding what to do with it is another. And that's what we're going to explore next.

Coping has been your survival mechanism. It's how you've managed the symptoms of the old story. It's what's kept you going all this time. But coping isn't freedom. Coping is survival. And healing? Healing is about addressing the story at its source. It's about rewriting it so it no longer runs your life.

The next step is to decide. Will you keep managing the symptoms, or will you go deeper and heal?

Reflective Questions

Let's take a moment to reflect:

- What are the recurring results in your life that frustrate you the most? Could they be tied to an old belief you've been carrying?
- If you could rewrite just one belief about yourself, what would it be?
- Who would you be without the story you've been living by? What would change if you let that story go?

Chapter 5

Coping vs. Healing

The Illusion of "I'm Fine"

In the last four chapters, we've taken a hard look at the stories running your life. We've uncovered what you've been chasing (peace, joy, success), what you've been running from (shame, rejection, fear), and how those patterns are rooted in the beliefs and self-image you've carried since childhood. By now, you've started to see how these old stories shape your thoughts, emotions, and decisions, keeping you in a cycle of striving, avoiding, and feeling stuck.

Even with all this awareness, there's a good chance you've convinced yourself, *"I'm fine."* Maybe you've told yourself that managing is enough—that coping is just a part of life. On the surface, it might even look like you've got it all together. You've figured out how to "make it work."

However, managing isn't healing—it's coping.

Coping is like having a trash can full of garbage sitting in your living room and learning how to deal with the smell. You light candles, buy expensive air fresheners, open the windows—anything to cover the odor. And after a while, you get so used to it that you barely notice it anymore. But the trash is still there, rotting away, and anyone who comes in can smell it immediately. That's what coping looks like—learning to live with the stink, hoping no one notices.

Healing, on the other hand, is like jumping in the trash can with Clorox on a Saturday morning, with Marvin Gaye playing and your mother standing behind you telling you, "You missed a spot!" and then pushing that trash can outside. It takes more courage, work and commitment—but when you're done, you're done. It's not about masking the discomfort; it's about confronting the source so it doesn't stink up your life anymore.

The first four chapters were about helping you *see* the trash can—identifying the stories, beliefs, and patterns that have been running your life. This chapter is about deciding what to do with it. Are you going to keep lighting candles and pretending everything's fine? Or are you ready to roll up your sleeves and take it out for good?

Why Coping Feels Safer

Why do we cling to coping? Because it feels safer than healing. Healing asks you to get your hands dirty. It asks you to face whatever you've been stuffing inside for years. And that kind of work? It's uncomfortable.

Coping *feels* easier because it lets you avoid the mess. It gives you a sense of control—like you're managing things, keeping it all together. The control isn't real. Coping lets you stay busy. It gives you something to do—light another candle, open another window, add another distraction. You tell yourself, *I'm fine. I've got this.* But deep down, you know that what you're really doing is running. Running from the smell, from the emotions that feel too overwhelming, from the stories you've never had the courage to face.

It's like spraying air freshener around that trash can in the living room. Sure, it masks the smell, but it doesn't eliminate the source. And over time, you adjust to the stink. You forget what fresh air feels like because you've convinced yourself that managing the smell is good enough.

Coping is survival mode disguised as control. It lets you feel productive without requiring you to do the deeper work. And that's the illusion—it tricks you into thinking you're handling things when all you're doing is avoiding them.

One thing about emotions is they don't go away just because you ignore them. They linger. They show up in your relationships, in your decisions, in the way you see yourself. And while coping lets you avoid the hard work of healing, it comes with a cost—a cost you're paying every single day. What's the price you're paying for holding it all together? What would happen if you stopped managing the symptoms and started addressing the root?

This is where coping becomes a trap. The longer you avoid the source, the heavier the weight becomes.

Coping doesn't just affect you—it leaks into every relationship and every interaction, shaping how you show up in the world. Picture that trash can in your living room. Now imagine someone walking in and saying, "*It stinks in here.*"

What's your first reaction? Defensive, right? *What smell? That's just how it is. Maybe you're too sensitive.*

You've lived with the smell for so long that you've forgotten it's even there. You're not reacting to the trash—you're reacting to their discomfort with the trash. And instead of seeing the garbage for what it is, you might start thinking, "*Why don't people just accept me for who I am?*"

It's not *you* they're rejecting—it's the unresolved emotions, unhealed wounds, and the baggage that you've been avoiding. The trash in your living room is stinking up the space, but because you're used to it, you assume the problem is everyone else.

Coping in relationships works the same way. When you carry unresolved baggage, it affects how you connect with others. You protect yourself from rejection, judgment, or pain by keeping your walls up, but those walls also keep out love, joy, and intimacy. You might tell yourself, "*They just don't understand me,*" when in reality, you haven't let them see the real you because you're afraid of what they'll think.

Think about it. If you've built your relationships around coping—managing emotions instead of addressing them—you're not really showing up as your full self. You're showing up as someone who's surviving, not thriving. That might look like:

- Getting defensive when someone points out a flaw because it triggers an old story of not being good enough.
- Avoiding difficult conversations because you don't want to risk rejection or conflict.
- Seeking validation from others while secretly doubting their love or approval.

Coping convinces you that you're protecting yourself, but what you're really doing is blocking the connection you crave. And when the relationship inevitably feels distant or strained, it reinforces the belief you've been carrying all along: *I'm not worthy of love.* But it's not the relationship that's broken—it's the weight of unresolved baggage shaping how you see it.

Let's take this a step further. Coping isn't just about relationships—it's about how you carry yourself in every area of life. It's like walking through the world with a backpack full of rocks. At first, you're aware of the weight, but over time, you adjust. You tell yourself, "*This is just how life is—heavy, hard, and exhausting.*"

The weight doesn't go away just because you've gotten used to it. It slows you down. It makes every step harder. And because it's been there for so long, you start to believe it's just a part of who you are.

Here's what that weight might look like in real life:

- Struggling to celebrate achievements because you're too busy bracing for the next challenge.
- Feeling disconnected in relationships, even when people are showing up for you.
- Burning out because every goal feels like an uphill battle.

Coping tricks you into thinking you're handling it, but in reality, you're just surviving. And the longer you carry that weight, the more it drains your energy, narrows your focus, and reinforces the idea that life is meant to be hard.

So, let me ask you, what's the trash can in your life? What unresolved emotions, beliefs, or stories have you been avoiding? What's the weight you've gotten so used to that you've forgotten it's even there?

This is the cost of coping. It keeps you stuck in survival mode, managing symptoms instead of addressing the source. The good news is the trash can doesn't have to stay there. The backpack doesn't have to stay on your shoulders. You can put it down. But first, you have to face it.

Mental Punishment: The Long Way Out

When I was a kid, my sister and I got into a fight, and I punched her in the stomach. She ran straight to my dad, who gave me a choice: take a whooping and go back out and play or stay grounded in my room for 30 days. Now, to my young mind, the choice was obvious. A butt whooping sounded terrible, but staying in my room? Easy. I could handle that.

Except I couldn't.

By the end of the first day, I realized I'd made a massive mistake. My family was out having the time of their lives—going to the movies, getting ice cream, laughing at jokes I couldn't hear. And I was stuck, alone in my room, missing all of it. After 24 hours of staring at the walls, I was ready to beg my dad to change his mind. "Just give me the whooping," I pleaded. But the decision was final—I was grounded, and I had to deal with it.

Looking back, that story is the perfect metaphor for what coping feels like. When you choose to cope instead of heal, you're putting yourself on mental punishment. You're locking yourself away from the fullness of life, telling yourself it's safer this way, easier this way. But it's not. It's lonely, exhausting, and never-ending. And just like my childhood grounding, it's all self-imposed.

The truth is, healing might feel like the harder option, but it's the quickest path to freedom. It's like taking the whooping—you face the pain head-on, and then it's over. The sting fades, and you're free to move on. Coping, on the other hand, drags the process out indefinitely. It keeps you stuck in a cycle of avoidance, while life happens without you.

So, let me ask you, how long have you been putting yourself on punishment? How many years have you spent managing the symptoms instead of addressing the source? How much longer are you willing to sit in that room, watching the world go on without you?

Coping feels safe, but it's the long way out. Healing might scare you, but it's the only way to step back into the life you were meant to live. The freedom you're looking for is on the other side of the emotional work you've been avoiding. And the sooner you face it, the sooner you'll realize that what you were afraid of wasn't nearly as bad as you thought. It never is.

What Healing Really Looks Like

I want you to imagine you going into your child's room and seeing them scared, hiding under the covers, shaking and holding a baseball bat. You ask them what's wrong and they point to the closet door saying, "There's a monster in the closet!" As an adult, you know there is no monster in the closet. To your child, that monster is absolutely in there and they are too afraid to even open the door and look.

Healing is like opening the closet where your childhood monsters still hide. For years, you've avoided that door, terrified of what's inside. To the child in you, the monster feels massive—looming, terrifying, all-consuming. But as an adult, when you finally open the door, you see it for what it really is: shadows and a coat hanging on a hook. Fear only has power because you haven't looked. As long as you never open that door, the monster will still feel real.

Healing doesn't mean reliving the pain. It means revisiting the story you created as a child—this time with the wisdom and perspective you have as an adult. Back then, you didn't have the tools to make sense of what happened. You were like a kid trying to put together a 1,000-piece puzzle with only 10 pieces in front of you. The picture you created wasn't wrong—it was just incomplete.

Healing is about picking up those missing pieces. It's about looking back at the stories you told yourself and asking, *"What else could this mean?"* Healing doesn't change the past, but it completely changes your perspective of the past. And when you change how you see the past, the present opens up in ways you never imagined.

Here's what healing looks like in practice:

- **In Relationships:** You stop bracing for rejection. Instead of overthinking every text or second-guessing every interaction, you feel grounded in who you are. Healing allows you to receive love without questioning if you deserve it and to give love without fear of being hurt. Disagreements stop feeling like threats, and intimacy becomes a safe space instead of a battlefield.
- **At Work:** You stop tying your worth to your performance. Criticism doesn't send you spiraling, and achievements don't feel like the only

way to prove your value. You can step into meetings, presentations, or new opportunities with confidence—not because you're perfect, but because you trust yourself. You're no longer hustling for validation; you're simply showing up as you.

- **With Yourself:** For the first time, you feel at peace just being you. You stop being at war with your own mind. The voice in your head that used to criticize, shame, or belittle you gets quieter. In its place, there's a sense of self-compassion. You forgive yourself for past mistakes, and you stop holding yourself to impossible standards. The constant hum of anxiety fades, and joy becomes easier to access. You laugh without wondering if you deserve to be happy. You rest without feeling guilty. You stop waiting for the other shoe to drop and start enjoying the moments you used to miss because you were too busy bracing for impact.

Healing doesn't make life perfect—it makes it real. It doesn't mean you'll never feel pain or struggle again. But it does mean that the pain won't control you anymore. It means you can experience emotions without being hijacked by them. It means you can respond to life instead of reacting to it.

When you heal, you're no longer running from your past or chasing validation in your present. You're free to create a life that feels light, joyful, and authentically yours. Imagine waking up and not dreading the day ahead. Imagine being able to breathe deeply, fully, without the weight of unspoken fears holding you down. That's what healing looks like.

The Bridge from Coping to Healing

In the last five chapters, we've been peeling back the layers of your life—revealing the beliefs, stories, and coping mechanisms that have shaped your self-image, dictated your decisions, and kept you stuck in a cycle of striving and surviving. You've uncovered what you've been chasing. You've confronted what you've been running from. And now, you're beginning to see that coping, while it may have helped you survive, isn't enough.

Coping has served its purpose—it got you here. But now it's time for something more. Healing isn't about looking back and feeling stuck in the pain of the past. It's about stepping into the truth of who you are. It's about reclaiming the joy, peace, and freedom that have always been your birthright.

Healing doesn't happen by accident. It takes intention, effort, and the right tools. That's where the *Eight Keys to Emotional Freedom* come in. These aren't abstract ideas or quick fixes—they're a step-by-step framework designed to help you rewrite the stories you've been living by, release the emotional weight you've been carrying, and finally break free from the cycles that have been running your life.

The hardest part—the decision to face yourself—has already been made. You're here, reading this, because you're ready. You're ready to stop running, stop managing, and start living. And I'm here to tell you that healing is possible. Not just for someone else, but for you.

Reflective Questions

Let's take a moment to reflect:

- What would your life look like if you let go of the stories holding you back?
- Who would you become if you stopped coping and started healing?

The **Eight Keys** are waiting. They are your roadmap to a life of emotional freedom, and they're up next.

Let's get to work.

Chapter 6

The Eight Keys to Emotional Freedom

What you're about to read might stir something inside you—curiosity, excitement, maybe even a little resistance. And that's okay. In fact, it's normal. If some of these ideas challenge the way you've always seen things, that was my intent and it just means you're exactly where you need to be. Growth always starts with a little discomfort.

These **Eight Keys** aren't about quick fixes or surface-level advice. They're not feel-good affirmations you'll forget by tomorrow. These are universal truths—clear, unshakable truths—that might feel hard to accept at first but have the power to change everything for you.

I've seen it happen. I've worked with people from every walk of life—from those carrying decades of unresolved trauma to high achievers who seem to "have it all" but feel empty inside. From convicted killers and drug dealers to CEOs of Fortune 500 companies and everything in between. I've served a multitude of ages, ethnicities, educational backgrounds, genders and people of different faiths. And no matter where they started, these keys have helped them uncover a level of emotional freedom they didn't think was possible. That's why I can say with confidence: if you're open to them, these keys will work for you, too.

Now, let me be upfront. Some of this might feel like tough pills to swallow. You might even find yourself pushing back, thinking, *"That can't be true for me."* That's just your old stories speaking, trying to keep you safe in familiar territory. But here's what I want you to remember as you keep reading: **you are not broken.** You've never been broken. The only thing in your way is the belief that something is wrong with you—and that belief is about to lose its power.

These keys aren't here to fix you. They're here to help you see what's been true all along: **you are already whole.** The work we're about to do isn't about changing who you are; it's about releasing the stories, beliefs, and patterns that have kept you from seeing yourself clearly.

This Process Is for Those Who Are Ready

The only thing that can block someone from experiencing true healing these keys have to offer, is their need to be right. If you're dead set on being right about the story you've been telling yourself—whether it's about your parents, your past, or your worth—these keys won't do much for you. But if you're ready, even just a little bit, to start questioning those stories, these keys can take you further than anything you've tried before.

I've had people come to me after trying everything—therapy, retreats, workshops, medication, meditation. You name it, they've done it. And yet, it was these keys—usually introduced during my breakthrough sessions or at group retreats—that cut straight through years of unresolved pain. I've watched people rewrite stories they thought were set in stone, stories tied to some of the deepest wounds you can imagine—rape, molestation, neglect, betrayal, abandonment. The kind of pain most people can't even talk about.

But here's what makes these keys so powerful: they don't just work in those extreme cases. They work for everyone. They uncover the same universal truths, whether someone is carrying the weight of unspoken trauma, the heartbreak of a failed relationship, or just that quiet, nagging feeling of never being enough. The beauty of these keys is that they don't change based on your story—they unlock freedom no matter what you've been through. The only question is whether you're ready to use them.

You May Not Agree at First

Now, I want to prepare you for something upfront—some of what you're about to read might hit a nerve. You might feel resistance bubbling up inside you. That's normal. It's part of the process. You see, the story you've been living by? It's been your survival strategy for years. It's what's helped you navigate life and protect yourself, so of course it feels hard to imagine letting it go. Real emotional freedom doesn't come from clinging to those old meanings. It comes from loosening your grip, one finger at a time.

These keys will challenge you. They'll ask you to look at your past, your relationships, and even yourself in ways you probably haven't before. They'll nudge you to open doors you've kept shut for years, to face the childhood stories you've buried, and to see the people who hurt you through a new lens.

I won't lie to you—this isn't easy work. It's a lot like peeling off armor you've worn for so long that you forgot it was there. That armor served a purpose, no doubt. But the freedom and peace waiting for you on the other side? It's worth every moment of discomfort. I promise you that.

My Invitation to You

I've seen people have life-changing breakthroughs with these keys in one-on-one sessions, but there's something magical about experiencing them in a group setting. When you're in a room full of people from different backgrounds—each carrying their own stories of pain—and you see these keys work across the board, it does something. You realize that you're not alone. And even more importantly, you realize that healing is possible.

The **Eight Keys** don't just offer insight—they offer freedom. But reading about them is one thing. Living them is another. That's why I encourage you to consider experiencing this work live. Whether it's at a retreat or a personal breakthrough session, the depth of transformation you'll experience is something words on a page can't fully capture.

The Eight Keys: A Gentle Introduction

We're going to take this slow. You won't get all eight keys thrown at you at once—because the truth is, each one takes time to digest. We'll reveal them one by one, layer by layer, giving you space to sit with each truth before moving on to the next.

Let me repeat, **this process isn't about fixing you—because you were never broken**. It's first about helping you see the stories you've been living by and then realizing they were never the whole truth.

You are already whole, always have been, and always will be. The keys you'll encounter are not about invalidating your pain but about offering you a new way to see your past and, more importantly, your future.

A Quick Note

As you read through each of these **Eight Keys**, remember this, you may not resonate with every story or example I use. You might read some and think, "That's not my experience" or "My life hasn't looked like that." And that's perfectly okay. The stories are here to show the power of each key, not to define your journey.

The key to getting the most out of this next section is to read these stories about **you.** I cannot stress this enough. If you read the stories as though they're only about the clients, you'll miss what there is to get for yourself.

What does that mean? It means that instead of focusing on the details of someone else's life, I want you to think about how these stories mirror your own. What emotions, patterns, or beliefs do you recognize in your own life? Ask yourself: Where have I been stuck like this? How does this apply to me? This book is not about these clients—**it's about you and your freedom.**

The truths behind these keys are universal—they're here to help you unlock freedom, regardless of the details of your past.

Whether your story involves a different kind of pain, a unique struggle, or even if it's more subtle, these keys still apply. Think of each story as a **lens** to see how these keys work in real lives. And trust that, no matter your experiences, the truths within these keys hold the same power for you, too.

One last thing, I want to encourage you to read these keys more than once. Make it a commitment to come back to them—not just once, but over and over—each time with a focus on you. Here's why: every time you read them, you'll have grown. You'll see things differently because you'll be different. And that means the keys will speak to you in new ways, revealing truths you might not have noticed the first time.

Think of it like revisiting a favorite book or movie—you notice something new every time because you've changed. These keys work the same way. So, give yourself permission to come back to them, again and again, letting them meet you wherever you are in your journey. The more you engage with them, the deeper their impact will be.

Putting the Kid Back on the Stand

Before we dive into the **Eight Keys**, let's revisit something we touched on earlier: the sham trial that shaped your self-image. Remember, this trial took place during your first 14 years of life, with a judge, jury, and executioner—all played by the child version of you. Every limiting belief you hold about yourself comes from this one-sided courtroom.

Back then, there were no defense attorneys, no cross-examinations and no one in your mental courtroom to argue on your behalf. Every decision you made about yourself was based on limited information, misunderstood events, and emotions too big for a kid to handle. You did the best you could with what you knew at the time, but without a proper trial, those verdicts have stayed with you, quietly dictating how you live today.

The purpose of the **Eight Keys** is to reopen that case—to put the little kid in you back on the witness stand, but this time with your adult mind present. **We're not here to erase the events of the past. We're here to reexamine the meanings (verdicts) you created about yourself as a result of those events.** It's time to cross-examine the story you've been telling yourself all these years.

What if those early conclusions weren't the truth? What if the people who hurt you were just acting out of their own feelings of brokenness? What if the love you thought you didn't receive was there all along—just not in the way you expected? What if the beliefs you've lived by were never meant to define you in the first place?

This process isn't about dismissing your experiences or minimizing your pain. **It's about giving yourself a fair trial for the first time**. It's about recognizing that the person you've been punishing (you) isn't guilty of the crimes you've accused them of. And the keys you're about to receive are the tools to unlock that mental prison—so you can finally set yourself free.

As we move through these next chapters, I invite you to stay open. Take your time with each key. Notice where you feel resistance—those moments are where the real work begins. Healing isn't about rushing through the process; it's about allowing yourself to be exactly where you are, without judgment.

So, grab a glass of water—because these pills might be hard to swallow. But on the other side of each one is freedom. And by the end of this journey, you'll understand that emotional freedom isn't something you have to chase—it's been waiting for you all along.

Chapter 7

Key # 1: It Wasn't About You

When you're a kid, everything feels personal. The way your parents acted, the things they said—or didn't say—it all felt like it was about you. If your dad missed birthdays, it meant you weren't worth the time. If your mom was depressed, it was because you weren't enough to make her happy. That's how we make sense of the world as children. We take it all in and say, *"This happened because of me."*

But the truth is, nothing anyone else did, parent or otherwise, was about you. None of it. Ever!

This is one of the hardest keys to unlock because it forces you to look back at your story with new eyes. It asks you to reconsider every moment when you felt unloved, abandoned, or not good enough and realize: it wasn't personal. Your parents had their own pain, their own struggles, and their own stories—just like you do now. What they did or didn't do wasn't a reflection of you. It was a reflection of them, of where they were in their journey, and of the tools they had at the time.

Meet Anna

Anna is, by all accounts, at the top of her game. As the CEO of a multi-million-dollar company, she'd achieved everything she thought would bring her peace and fulfillment. She was admired, respected, and known for her drive. She'd built her career from the ground up, made a name for herself, and reached the kind of success many people only dream about. Yet, sitting across from me that day, she confessed something that felt almost like a betrayal of her own accomplishments.

"Why doesn't any of this feel like enough?" she asked. "I have everything I thought I wanted, everything I thought would make me feel…worthy, I guess. And yet, there's this ache I can't get rid of. This feeling that, deep down, I'm still not enough. I can't stop wondering what's wrong with me."

We talked more about her life, her past, and eventually, it all came back to a familiar story. For Anna, it was rooted in her childhood—a time when she absorbed every painful moment and took it all personally. When her dad left, she made it mean that she wasn't worth staying for. When her mom was stressed and distant, Anna believed it was because she wasn't enough to make her mom happy. All these beliefs had shaped her drive, pushing her to succeed, to achieve, and to prove herself. But the success she'd chased for years couldn't silence the old, unhealed story: *If I had been enough, my parents would have stayed together, and would have been happy.*

"It's hard to imagine that it's not about me," she admitted. "It feels so personal."

I could see the weight of it in her eyes. To her, this wasn't just a story; it was the foundation of everything she'd been striving for her entire life. I knew this was a tough shift for her to make, and so I shared a story with her—one that I thought might help her see things differently.

The Kid in Solitary Confinement

I told Anna about a kid I'd met in a maximum-security prison. He was in solitary confinement, isolated from everyone else because his anger and pain were so intense that no one knew how to reach him. When the deputy warden came to me, desperate for help, they led me to his cell, and I spoke to him through the locked door. I shared my own story of loss, of things that didn't make sense, so he would know that whatever he was feeling, I could handle it.

After a while, he started to talk. I asked him, "Who did you crave love from the most?"

"My grandma," he said, almost instinctively.

"And what are you so angry about?" I asked.

He told me how his grandmother had struggled with addiction, how she'd overdosed and died. He believed, down to his core, that if she'd really loved him, she wouldn't have chosen drugs. She wouldn't have left him behind. He was so convinced that her choices were about him, a reflection of his worth.

"So, I get it," I told Anna. "I really do. But I asked him to consider a different perspective."

I shared with him that no one wakes up one day and says, "I want to become a drug addict." His grandmother hadn't chosen addiction over him; she'd been struggling with her own pain, her own feelings of brokenness. I asked him if he knew about her childhood, and he admitted that she'd gone through things he hadn't really considered—abuse, trauma, hardship.

"She wasn't using drugs because she didn't love you," I told him. "She was using drugs because she was trying to cope with her pain. She was trying to survive her own story and raise you at the same time."

As we continued to dive deeper into his grandmother's past, I could see the shift in his face, the way his whole body softened as these new insights set in. For the first time, he saw his grandmother not as a failed superhero, but as a human being—hurt, overwhelmed, and doing the best she could. And just like that, the anger he'd carried for years began to dissolve.

"It wasn't about me," he whispered.

"No," I said. "It never was."

As I told Anna this story, I could see her start to connect the dots. I could see it in the way her shoulders softened, her gaze steadied. She'd spent her life trying to outrun her limiting beliefs, to prove they weren't true, but now she was seeing that they'd never been true to begin with.

Just like the young man in solitary confinement, she'd been carrying the weight of her parent's actions, taking them as proof of her own worth—or lack thereof. This new shift for her was a huge relief.

A Gentle Note for Those Who've Experienced Sexual Trauma

If you've experienced sexual trauma—like I have—this key might feel especially hard to accept. Sexual abuse is profoundly personal, violating both body and soul. It can leave you feeling like your sense of safety, trust, and self-worth has been shattered. When someone hurts you in such an intimate way, it's easy to believe that their actions were about you—that it says something about who you are, what you deserve, or your value as a person.

But here's what I want you to hear, and hear deeply: It wasn't about you. Not then. Not now.

This isn't about excusing or absolving the person who hurt you. They are fully responsible for what they did. Nothing can change that. But the purpose of recognizing that it wasn't about you is to help you shift the meaning you may have created about yourself in the aftermath of that trauma.

Abuse has a way of planting deep-rooted beliefs— "I'm dirty," "I'm worthless," "I deserved this"—that run quietly in the background of your life, influencing your relationships, self-esteem, and decisions. These beliefs were never true, but they feel real because they took root when you were vulnerable, scared, and trying to make sense of something you couldn't understand.

I had to learn this for myself. For years, I carried the belief that what happened to me was somehow about me—something I did, something I didn't do, something I was. But as I began my own healing journey, I started to step back and see the situation from a broader perspective. I realized that the person who violated me wasn't acting out of anything to do with me. They were acting from their own pain, their own feelings of brokenness, and their own unmet needs.

When I asked myself, "What could have been going through their mind to make them think it was okay to do this to me?" I had to confront a hard truth: the person who hurt me only knew how to do that because someone must have done it to them. That cycle of pain didn't start with me—it was passed down.

This realization didn't come easily. It required a level of consciousness I wasn't sure I had. But when I could see the humanity in their actions—not excusing them, but understanding them—it changed something in me. I began to see that their actions were a cry for help, not a statement about my worth.

In *The Way of Mastery*, there's a powerful teaching: All human action is either an extension of love or a cry for help. Looking back, I realized that the person who hurt me was just a kid himself. And if he was doing something like that to me at such a young age, someone must have done it to him. He didn't fully understand what he was doing. I could see that he wasn't just acting out of malice—he was acting out of deep pain, searching for something he didn't know how to find.

Today, I still see him from time to time. He's addicted to drugs and lost in his own world. I don't feel anger when I see him—I feel compassion. Not because what he did was okay, but because I can see that he's still carrying a weight he doesn't know how to release.

That situation wasn't about me. It wasn't personal. I was involved, but I wasn't the *cause*.

I know this is an incredibly hard pill to swallow, but if you desire peace, it's one that must be swallowed. No one's actions are about you, just like your actions aren't about anyone else. And this is an important distinction: Even when someone's actions impact you deeply, it's not about you.

Let me give you another example. Imagine I said to you that I'm going to spend the rest of my life and all of my resources to make your life absolutely miserable. Is that about you or is that about me? Yes, you are involved, but the question is, is my desire to make you miserable about you or about me? Of course, it's about me. It's about me because deep down, there's something inside me that's convinced that in order for me to feel good about my life, I have to make you suffer.

It's the same with the person who hurt you. Their actions weren't about you. They were about their own inner turmoil, their own distorted beliefs, their own pain.

Once you let go of the belief that the abuse defined you, you begin to reclaim your story. What happened to you was an event—it doesn't get to decide who you are or how your life unfolds moving forward.

By releasing the weight of their actions, you give yourself the freedom to see the truth: **You are whole.** You are worthy. And what happened to you doesn't get to write the ending of your story—you do.

Everyone Is the Star of Their Own Movie

To drive this point home, I explained to Anna that each of us is the star of our own movie. Our experiences, our stories—they're all filtered through our own perspective. But everyone else is starring in their own movie, too. In their lives, we're just extras in the background.

"When you're driving on the road," I said, "all those other cars? They're just part of your scenery, part of your journey. But in their world, you're the extra. You're just another car on the road. That's how life is—everyone is so wrapped up in their own stories, their own survival. Your parents were no different. They were trying to navigate their own lives, and what they did or didn't do wasn't a reflection of you."

I watched as this idea sank in, as Anna began to let go of the belief that she'd somehow been at the center of her parents' pain or choices. Her parents, like the rest of us, were navigating life through their own lens.

The Emotional Driver Behind Actions

Everything you do—yes, everything—is driven by one of two motives: to gain a feeling you desire or to avoid a feeling you fear. Let that sink in for a moment. Every decision, action, or behavior you've ever made boils down to chasing or dodging an emotion.

Think about it. Why do you work so hard at your job? Is it really just for the paycheck, or is it because you want to feel secure, accomplished, or respected? Why do you avoid certain conversations? Is it because you're busy, or is it because you're trying to avoid discomfort, rejection, or conflict? Everything you do is tied to a feeling we're trying to get or a feeling you'd rather not deal with.

Now, let's flip this lens outward. If everything you do is driven by your emotional needs, doesn't it make sense that the same is true for everyone else? When someone hurts you, disappoints you, or doesn't show up in the way you hoped, it's not about you—it's about *them* trying to manage their own feelings.

Let's go back to Anna's story. When her dad left, she internalized it as a reflection of her worth. But the truth? Her dad wasn't thinking about Anna when he walked out the door. He was consumed by his own emotional storm—maybe fear of failure, maybe shame, maybe a desperate need to escape his life. Or maybe her parents just didn't like each other anymore. Regardless of the reason, his actions weren't about Anna; they were about him trying to avoid a feeling he couldn't handle.

The same goes for Anna's mom. Her emotional distance wasn't a critique of Anna's lovability. It was her way of coping with the overwhelming stress and sadness she felt. Her actions were a reflection of her own attempts to manage her emotional world, not a statement about Anna.

What This Means for You

This isn't just about understanding other people—it's about understanding yourself. Think about the times you've snapped at someone, withdrawn from a relationship, or made a choice you later regretted. Were you really thinking about the other person in those moments? Or were you trying to navigate your own emotional landscape? Maybe you were feeling overwhelmed, scared, or unworthy, and your actions were an attempt to gain or avoid a specific feeling.

If this is true for you, why would it be any different for others? The truth is, it's not. People are operating from their own emotional needs, fears, and desires—just like you. Their actions are rarely, if ever, about you.

Let's make this practical. Here's how this dynamic might be playing out in your life right now:

- **At Work:** When a colleague undermines you, you think it's because they don't like you. But what if it's their own insecurity, their need to feel important, or their fear of being overshadowed that's driving their behavior?
- **In Relationships:** When your partner shuts down during an argument, you take it as a sign that they don't care. But what if they're overwhelmed and trying to avoid feelings of inadequacy or fear of conflict?

- **With Family:** When a parent criticizes you, you interpret it as disappointment. But what if they're projecting their own regrets, their own unmet expectations, or their need to feel in control?

Notice the pattern? Other people's actions are almost always about them and their feelings—not you.

You're not exempt from this truth. Just like everyone else, your actions are driven by your emotional needs. When you overwork, is it really about ambition, or are you trying to avoid feelings of inadequacy? When you avoid conflict, is it about keeping the peace, or are you dodging the discomfort of rejection or confrontation?

This is where self-awareness becomes your superpower. When you start to see how your own behaviors are tied to your emotional drivers, you can begin to break free from the cycle of blaming yourself for other people's actions. Because if their behavior isn't about you, and your behavior isn't about them, you can finally stop personalizing everything and start focusing on what's really going on beneath the surface.

The Freedom of Letting Go

Here's the beauty of this realization: when you stop taking other people's actions personally, you free yourself from a burden that was never yours to carry. You can start seeing their behavior for what it is—a reflection of their inner world, not a commentary on your worth.

And when you apply this same lens to yourself, you can begin to unravel the emotional patterns that are driving your own choices. You can ask yourself, *"What am I really trying to gain or avoid here?"* and make decisions from a place of clarity instead of reaction.

The next time someone lets you down, hurts you, or behaves in a way that feels unfair, pause for a moment. Ask yourself, *"What feeling might they be trying to gain or avoid?"* And then remind yourself: *It's not about me.*

The Shift That Sets You Free

This key—*It Wasn't About You*—isn't about excusing the hurt you've experienced. It's about releasing yourself from the belief that you were the cause of it. It's about freeing yourself from the mistaken belief that other people's actions were a measure of your value. People act from their own wounds, their own pain, and their own stories. Recognizing that sets you free.

The kid in the juvenile facility let go of his anger when he saw his grandmother's addiction for what it was: a symptom of her pain, not a measure of her love.

As Anna and I continued to work through her stories from the first 14 years of her life, she began to see that her parents' choices not only didn't define her worth; they were simply reflections of her parent's mental and emotional states at the time. In that moment, as she released the belief that she wasn't enough, a lifetime of resentment and striving for worthiness began to loosen its hold.

"It wasn't about me," she whispered.

Anna's Life After the Breakthrough

Today, Anna approaches life with a sense of freedom she never thought possible. She's still the CEO, still achieving, but her motivation has shifted. She no longer feels like she's running from her past or trying to prove her worth. Instead, she's connected to a new sense of purpose, one that isn't tied to anyone else's actions or approval. Her success has become something she enjoys rather than something she uses to fill an invisible void.

This shift has transformed her relationships as well. She's more present with her team and her family, and she no longer carries the weight of needing others' validation. Her inner peace isn't dependent on what she accomplishes or how others perceive her. Instead, she knows her worth, independent of any achievement. She's found a genuine joy that's rooted in who she is—not in the things she's done.

With this new freedom, Anna describes feeling like she's finally in her own story, not someone else's. She's let go of old resentments and beliefs that once held her back, and she's showing up in the world as the person she's always been beneath the layers. She no longer feels the need to play a role or wear a mask; she's simply Anna—whole, worthy, and finally at peace with herself.

Reflective Questions

Take a moment to reflect:

- What moments in your past have you made about you, believing they defined your worth?
- How have these moments shaped your drive, your relationships, your choices?
- What would it feel like to let go of the idea that these moments were about you?
- What emotions have been driving your recent choices—both the ones you're proud of and the ones you're not?
- Can you think of a time when someone's actions hurt you? What feelings might they have been trying to manage in that moment?
- How would your life change if you stopped personalizing other people's behavior and started focusing on your own emotional drivers instead?

This is just the beginning.

As we move forward through each key, remember: you're peeling back layers, uncovering truths that may have been buried for years. Just like Anna, you'll soon see yourself—and your past—through a completely new lens.

Let's keep going.

Chapter 8

Key #2: It Had Nothing to Do with You

As a child, you had a way of inserting yourself into situations that had nothing to do with you. You'd see something happen—a tense moment, an argument, or a parent's bad day—and immediately felt obligated to do something about it or make it better. Not because you were self-centered, but because, in your world, everything felt connected to you. You didn't have the perspective to step back and say, *"This isn't my responsibility."* So instead, you absorbed it. You internalized it. You started creating stories in your own head like, *"This must be my fault somehow."*

Here's where this key differs from *It Wasn't About You.* That first key is about letting go of the belief that people's actions—especially the hurtful ones—were a reflection of your value or worth. This key, *It Had Nothing to Do With You,* focuses on how you made other people's situations your responsibility, even when they weren't. You didn't just take it personally; you took it on even though it wasn't your load to bear.

The problem is, none of it was ever your job to fix. But because you were nosy and made it your business, you started creating beliefs about who you are and what you're responsible for based on things that had nothing to do with you in the first place. And those beliefs? They didn't stay in childhood. They followed you, shaping how you see yourself, how you show up, and how you try to control or manage everything around you. All because you took on roles and burdens that were never meant for you.

Meet David

David, a senior manager in the tech industry, came to me carrying a heavy burden—a story he'd held onto for over 30 years. Although successful and respected in his field, David felt unfulfilled and disconnected in his personal life. He was going through a divorce and struggling to understand why he kept sabotaging his relationships, always holding himself back from fully committing.

As he shared his story, it became clear that his struggles stemmed from a belief he had formed as a young boy. When he was just eight years old, he watched his mother move out of the house. In his mind, she didn't just leave the house; she left *him*. For decades, he carried this story: *If my mother loved me, she wouldn't have left. If I were enough, she would have stayed or taken me with her.*

This belief followed him like a shadow into every relationship, every moment of doubt, every time he felt like he didn't measure up. Despite all his achievements and the admiration he received from others, he constantly heard that whisper, *"You weren't enough for your own mother to stay."*

I asked him a question he hadn't considered, "What was happening in your mom's life when she left?"

At first, he seemed taken aback. "What do you mean? She left *me*. That's all I've ever thought about."

I encouraged him to go deeper, to try seeing the situation not through the eyes of the hurt little boy but from the perspective of an adult who might be struggling. I gave him a task to go find out from his mother's siblings, not only everything going on during that time, but everything his mother experienced growing up. This was important because without the understanding of what his mother had been through, he would never understand her actions. About a week later he came back and shared how he now recognized that his mother's actions had nothing to do with him and had everything to do with her own pain, her own challenges.

This uncovered a liberating truth: His mother wasn't leaving *him*. She was escaping an abusive relationship and didn't have the mental or emotional capacity to care for him properly, and knew that taking him along would put both of them at even greater risk. She wasn't leaving because he wasn't enough—she was leaving because she was fighting for her life.

Three Sides to Every Story: Your Side, Their Side, and the Truth

When I was eight years old, my mother dropped me off at my grandmother's house. I didn't think much of it—I figured she'd be back the next day to pick me up. But instead, this guy shows up claiming to be my father. I hadn't seen him much before that, so the situation was already confusing. Then he hit me with the line that would echo in my head for decades: *"I'm taking you to live with me. Your mom doesn't want you anymore."*

Let me tell you, that hit hard. My eight-year-old brain didn't know what to do with it except take it as the truth. My mom didn't want me. She abandoned me. The person who was supposed to love me most in the world had just...given me up.

I didn't have the tools to question it or the perspective to see anything beyond what I was told. And just like that, I started building a story in my head—a story that would shape my relationships, my behavior, and my sense of worth for the next 20 years.

That story? It led me to resent my mother, deeply. I resented her for leaving me, and I resented my grandmother for letting it happen. Worst of all, it showed up in how I treated women. I couldn't trust them. I pushed them away before they had the chance to leave me. I held on to this anger, this pain, because in my mind, my mom didn't care enough to stick around.

Then, when I was 28 years old, I learned the other side of the story. And let me tell you, it shook me to my core.

Turns out, my mother never abandoned me. What actually happened was a whole situation orchestrated by my grandmother and my father. My dad went behind my mom's back to gain full custody of me. Once the court ruling came through, my grandmother called my mom to drop me off at her house, then immediately called my dad to come pick me up. When my mom came back to get me, I was already gone.

Let that sink in for a second. The story I had been telling myself for 20 years—that my mother didn't want me—wasn't even close to the truth. My mom didn't abandon me. She fought for me. She was devastated. But no one explained that to an eight-year-old kid. No one gave me the full picture. So, I did what kids do: I filled in the gaps with the most logical story I could come up with at the time.

And that story? It was a lie.

It took me 20 years to find out the truth, but by then, the damage was already done. I had spent two decades living out the consequences of a story that wasn't even real.

We all have a story. And in that story, we're the star. We see the events of our lives through our own eyes, shaped by our emotions, experiences, and the beliefs we've carried for years. It's natural to think that our perspective is the *right* perspective—after all, it's the only one we've lived. Every story has at least three sides. There's your side, their side, and somewhere in between lies the truth.

Think about it like this, you're standing on one side of a room, and someone else is on the opposite side. In the middle is a giant vase. From your angle, the vase might look like it's decorated with flowers, but from their side, they see geometric patterns. You're both describing the same vase, but your perspectives are completely different. Neither of you is wrong—you're just seeing it from angles the other person can't. And the truth? It's not one perspective or the other. The truth is the vase, which holds both designs at the same time.

Now, let's apply this to your life. When you think back on a situation—whether it's an argument, a childhood event, or a moment that left a lasting scar—you're likely viewing it from *your* angle. That's not wrong, but it's incomplete. There's another angle, another perspective you might not have considered.

Take a moment to think about someone you've been in conflict with. From your side, they were wrong—they didn't listen, they hurt you, they didn't care. But have you ever stopped to wonder how it looked from their side? What if their actions weren't about hurting you at all, but were a reflection of their own pain, fears, or misunderstandings? What if they, too, were carrying their own beliefs and stories that colored their view of what happened?

This doesn't mean their side is right and yours is wrong. It simply means there's more to the story than what you've been telling yourself.

When you're only looking at your side, you might be missing valuable context that can help you heal, grow, or even forgive. For example, let's say your parents were emotionally distant when you were growing up. From your perspective, they didn't love you enough, or maybe they didn't care. But what was going on in their world? Were they struggling with their own unhealed trauma? Were they overwhelmed, scared, or simply doing the best they could with the tools they had?

Understanding that there are multiple sides to every story doesn't mean you have to excuse hurtful behavior. It doesn't let anyone off the hook for their actions. What it does is expand your view, allowing you to see the situation with greater clarity and compassion.

Shifting Your Perspective

The truth often lies somewhere in the middle—not in a "split the difference" kind of way, but in a way that honors the complexity of human experience. It's rarely black and white. Instead, it's a mix of intention, perception, and circumstance.

When you're willing to step back and ask yourself, *"What might I be missing?"* you open the door to a deeper understanding. Maybe your parents didn't know how to show love because they'd never been shown love themselves. Maybe that friend who stopped calling wasn't rejecting you—they were overwhelmed by their own life. Maybe the person who hurt you wasn't trying to break you—they were acting from their feelings of brokenness.

So how do you start seeing the bigger picture? By challenging your narrative. The next time you feel certain about a situation, pause and ask yourself:

- What might this look like from the other person's perspective?
- What might they have been feeling or experiencing in that moment?
- Is it possible that their actions had nothing to do with me?

This doesn't mean you have to agree with their side or invalidate your own feelings. It simply means you're willing to entertain the idea that there's more to the story than what you've been telling yourself.

Your side is valid. Their side is valid. But the full picture, the *truth*, is often something greater than either perspective alone. And when you can step into that middle ground, you give yourself the freedom to let go of resentment, judgment, and pain that may no longer serve you.

The vase isn't just flowers or patterns—it's both. Life isn't just your perspective or theirs—it's all of it. And in understanding that, you create space for healing, compassion, and, ultimately, peace.

To help David further understand how our childhood beliefs can shape our adult lives, I shared a story about another client I'd worked with—a 31-year-old woman who had spent years avoiding close relationships. When we traced her story back, it led to a memory from when she was just five years old. One day on the playground, her best friend suddenly ran off to play with another group of kids without saying a word. That was it—a small moment in the grand scheme of things. But to the five-year-old her, it was devastating. She created a belief that people can't be trusted and that closeness leads to betrayal. That single moment shaped her relationships for the next 26 years.

David could see the connection. "So that little girl created a whole story around that one moment?" he asked.

"Yes," I replied, "and so did you."

When the Story Feels Personal—But Isn't

As you read this from an adult's perspective, the idea that someone else's actions had nothing to do with you might seem obvious. Of course, your mom's struggles weren't about you. Of course, your parents' fights or divorce weren't your fault. But in a child's mind, everything feels personal. And that's because children don't think with logic—they think with emotion.

This is crucial to understand. As a child, your brain is still developing and hasn't gained the ability to see the world from multiple perspectives yet. You are living in a highly emotional, self-centered state, which means everything you experience feels like it revolves around you. If someone leaves, it must be because *you* did something wrong. If your parents fight, it must be because *you* weren't good enough to keep the peace.

As David and I explored this idea, he began to see how, as a child, he had misunderstood his mother's struggles. It wasn't his fault. Her leaving had nothing to do with him. And yet, this story had shaped his entire life.

How We Fill in the Gaps with False Narratives

Here's the thing about memory, science tells us that most of our memories are incomplete, and our brains fill in the gaps with whatever makes the most sense to us. Psychologists distinguish between two types of memory—episodic memory, which stores the details of events, and somatic memory, which holds general knowledge and facts. When we try to recall specific moments from childhood, we often reconstruct those memories by pulling from both types. The problem? We don't always get it right.

To explain the concept of *episodic memory* versus *somatic memory* and how we fill in the gaps, let's consider a question you may have heard before: *Where were you on 9/11?*

You might immediately recall where you were, who you were with and what you were doing when you first heard the news. Maybe you remember the color of the sky, the way your stomach dropped, or the look on someone's face. The catch is that every time you recall that memory, you're not pulling it from some untouched archive in your brain. Instead, you're recreating it, piece by piece, like a puzzle. And every time you recreate it, the details shift slightly based on your current state of mind, emotions, or what you've heard since then.

Maybe you weren't watching TV when the news broke, but over the years, you've seen so many news clips that you're convinced you were glued to the screen that morning. Maybe the conversation you remember having that day didn't happen until a week later. The core of the memory might be accurate, but the details you've filled in? Those might be completely made up. This is how episodic memory works—it's prone to edits and revisions every time you access it.

Now let's contrast this with *somatic memory*—the physical sensations your body holds onto, even if you can't recall the exact events. For example, let's say you had a tense relationship with one of your parents growing up. You might not remember specific arguments or moments of disappointment, but your body remembers the tightness in your chest, the sinking feeling in your stomach, or the way your muscles would tense when they raised their voice.

When you try to piece together *why* you feel this way as an adult, your brain might fill in the gaps with stories to match those sensations—stories that might not be entirely accurate. Maybe you think, *"They were disappointed in me because I wasn't good enough."* But in reality, their frustration could've been about their own stress or struggles, not you. Your brain connected the dots the best it could at the time, but those dots were based on incomplete information.

This is what we mean by filling in the gaps. Your brain's job is to make sense of the world, even when the facts aren't clear. And sometimes, the stories it comes up with are just that—stories. They feel real because they're tied to your emotions, but that doesn't make them true. The problem is, we carry these stories forward, letting them shape how we see ourselves and the world, without ever questioning whether they're accurate in the first place.

For David, his brain filled in those gaps with the assumption that he wasn't worthy of love—that he wasn't enough. This interpretation colored everything he did, from his personal relationships to his career, reinforcing the belief that he was somehow to blame.

I encouraged David to look back on those early years with fresh eyes, reminding him that his inner child had been working with limited information. As an adult, though, he had the power to re-examine these memories with greater understanding and compassion.

Revisiting these childhood memories can feel unsettling at first because they've been so tightly woven into the fabric of your identity. The uncertainty that comes from imagining who you would be without the story that you have told yourself for so long can feel scary or overwhelming.

These beliefs have lived with you for so long that they've shaped how you see yourself and the world around you. But the beauty of this process is that it allows you to question what you've always taken as truth. Because the actual truth is **you were already whole, always have been, always will be.**

As David worked through this, he realized that the belief he'd held for so long wasn't necessarily true. *What if my mother leaving wasn't a statement about my worth?* This was the beginning of emotional freedom for him—a chance to live without the shadow of that false narrative.

Letting Go of False Narratives

David's story isn't unique. You might not have the same details, but the pattern? Oh, it's all too familiar. Somewhere along the line, you decided someone else's pain, someone else's problem, or someone else's choices were somehow your responsibility. You didn't just notice their struggles—you made them about *you*. And just like David, you've been lugging that story around like a suitcase full of bricks ever since.

So, what does this look like in your life? Maybe you're the overachiever who feels like you can never do enough, because if you're not "on," everything falls apart. Or maybe you're the one who avoids relationships, terrified deep down that you'll be abandoned, so you figure it's easier not to even try. Or perhaps you've spent years chasing success, believing that if you finally hit that elusive goal, it'll prove your worth to...well, who exactly? Your inner eight-year-old?

Here's the truth you need to hear: *It had nothing to do with you.* Whatever burden you picked up as a child, it wasn't yours to carry. Your parents' struggles? Not yours. Their bad days, their shouting matches, their inability to show up? None of it was your fault. None of it was your responsibility. You weren't a player in their game; you were just caught in the crossfire.

For David, it wasn't enough to understand his mother's struggles on an intellectual level. He had to confront the belief he created in that moment: *She left because I wasn't worth staying for.* That belief had shaped his entire life, coloring every relationship with fear and insecurity.

The same is true for you. It's not enough to intellectually know that your parents did the best they could with what they had. You also have to change the meaning you gave those experiences and the belief you created about yourself as a result. This is the secret sentence running your life—hidden just beneath the surface, quietly influencing every decision you make, every relationship you build, and every dream you chase. And because these are beliefs quietly running in the background you create your own suffering and then play victim to your own creations.

A Shift That Sets You Free

You've been living your life as though those childhood stories were gospel truth. You've let them define how you see yourself, how you show up, and how you operate in the world. But what if—and this is big—those stories were never about you? What if the narrative you've been clinging to is nothing more than a distorted version of events told by a kid who didn't know better?

Imagine the freedom of realizing that your mom leaving wasn't because you weren't good enough—it was because she couldn't handle her own pain. Imagine understanding that your dad's anger wasn't about you—it was about his own unhealed wounds. Imagine waking up tomorrow and feeling the weight lift as you finally accept: *It had nothing to do with me.*

Here's your aha moment. Those stories you've carried for years? They're just that—stories. They were your brain's best attempt to make sense of the chaos, but they're not the truth. And the meaning you assigned to those events as a child? It doesn't serve you anymore. It's time to let it go.

Picture this, you, standing tall, free from the weight of someone else's baggage. You, showing up in the world not as someone trying to prove their worth but as someone who already knows they're whole. Because that's what you are—whole, worthy, and free.

Now, tell me—what's stopping you from setting it down? Because the only person keeping that weight on your shoulders is you. It's time to rewrite the story. It's time to let go.

David's Life After the Breakthrough

When David began to see his mother's actions for what they truly were—a reflection of her struggles, not his worth—he felt a shift within himself. He recognized that he didn't have to carry the weight of that belief anymore. He accepted that letting go of these false narratives wasn't about excusing people's behavior or pretending the pain didn't happen but it's about reclaiming his power. He understood that it's about recognizing that the meaning he assigned to those events as a child no longer serves him as an adult.

As David let go of that story, he found a new sense of freedom—a way of being in relationships that wasn't governed by fear and self-doubt. For the first time, he could see himself as worthy of love and connection, without the need to protect himself with emotional walls.

Reflective Questions

Let's take a moment to reflect:

- Are there moments from your childhood that you've made about you—moments that had nothing to do with you?
- What belief did you create about yourself as a result of those experiences?
- How has that belief shaped your life, your relationships, and your sense of self?
- What would it feel like to let go of the idea that it was ever about you?

Chapter 9

Key #3: It Was None of Your Business

There's a weight so many of us carry, often without even realizing it—the weight of responsibilities, worries, and expectations that were never ours to begin with. Most of us picked it up as kids, convinced we somehow had the power—and duty—to fix everything wrong in the world around us. Sounds crazy when you say it out loud, doesn't it? But here we are, still lugging it around.

Think about it, when you were a kid, you didn't have the perspective to step back and say, *"This isn't my problem."* Instead, you saw your parents arguing, struggling, or silently stressed out, and your brain jumped to conclusions. *"Maybe if I were better, quieter, smarter, or easier to deal with, they'd be okay."* You took on roles you didn't ask for: the fixer, the caretaker, the peacemaker. No one handed you that job description—you just assumed it was yours.

Now, imagine your own child overhearing you vent about a tough day at work. The next day, they come to you with a detailed plan to "fix" your stress. You'd probably laugh and say, "Sweetheart, that's not your job. I've got this." But did anyone ever tell you that? Did anyone look you in the eyes and say, "This isn't your weight to carry"? Probably not. So, you carried it anyway, believing that if you were just "enough," you could make everything better.

Here's the truth, whatever you are carrying from back then, it was never your business. Just like you'd reassure your own child, I'm telling you now—set it down. You were a kid, playing a small part in the lives of the adults around you. But somewhere along the way, you convinced yourself that you were the star of their stories too, responsible for making sure everything worked out. You weren't. And clinging to that role isn't heroic—it's exhausting.

Meet Jessica

Jessica is a highly successful real estate broker, known for her relentless drive and commitment. She handled every detail meticulously, always on the go. Her mind never stopped, her body rarely rested, and her thoughts constantly raced from one task to the next. Fatigue had become her constant companion, and she'd begun experiencing health issues that she could no longer ignore. Yet, Jessica didn't know how to rest; even the idea of taking a break made her feel guilty. She felt as though slowing down somehow meant failing.

"Jessica," I asked during our first session, "when was the last time you allowed yourself to truly rest without feeling like you were dropping the ball?"

She hesitated, her eyes drifting downward. "Honestly? I can't remember," she admitted. "It's like… if I'm not doing everything, I feel like I'm letting people down. And if I let them down, it feels like I'm failing."

Despite her outward success, Jessica felt burdened by an unspoken fear: if she didn't keep everything together, who would? She held this weight on her shoulders alone and thought it was her responsibility to manage it all. As we dug deeper, I sensed her need for control was more than just a habit—it was something deeply rooted in a belief she'd held since childhood.

When We Take On What Was Never Ours to Carry

As we talked, I guided Jessica back to her earliest memories to explore when she might have first felt this drive to hold everything together. She described nights lying awake as a child, listening to her parents' tense conversations about money. She could remember the worry in her mother's voice and how she'd sometimes see her mom crying quietly, trying to keep her fears hidden.

"I just remember thinking, if I could do well in school, help out more at home, maybe they wouldn't be so worried," she said softly. "I thought that if I was good enough, maybe I could make things better for them."

"And that's where it all began," I said. "As a child, you absorbed that stress, feeling like you had to make everything okay. But the truth is, none of that was your business to begin with. You eavesdropped on a conversation and made what wasn't your business or responsibility your business and responsibility and created all of this unnecessary stress as a result."

"Imagine," I continued, "your child eavesdropped on a conversation between you and your husband and later came to you and said, 'Mommy I heard you and daddy's conversation the other night and came up with a list of things I can do to take the stress off of you both', how would you respond?" Immediately she replied, "I'd tell her to stop listening in on our conversation and mind her own business. I'd tell her that what she heard had nothing to do with her."

"Exactly," I replied. "How you would correct your child in that moment is how I'm correcting you now."

Jessica's eyes filled with a mix of realization and sorrow. She was beginning to understand that this need to control every aspect of her life had its roots in a story she'd been telling herself since childhood—a story that convinced her she had to hold everything together for the people around her.

Control: The Illusion of Safety

For Jessica, control wasn't just a habit—it was a survival strategy, deeply rooted in her childhood chaos. She believed that if she could just manage everything and everyone, she could prevent bad things from happening.

Let's pause there. Sound familiar? Control often feels like the ultimate safety net, doesn't it? Like if you can just stay ahead of every curveball, predict every outcome, and micromanage every detail, you'll somehow be untouchable. But let me break it to you gently—or maybe not so gently: that's complete nonsense.

The truth is control is an illusion—a seductive, anxiety-fueled illusion. The belief that you can control the uncontrollable is like thinking you can stop the tide with a bucket. Sure, you might scoop up some water here and there, but the ocean's going to do what the ocean does. And life? It's no different.

So where does this desperate need to control everything come from? Fear. Plain and simple. Control is fear wearing a disguise, convincing you that if you can just get a handle on everything *"around you,"* you won't have to deal with the uncertainty *"within you"*.

As a child, when things felt chaotic—parents arguing, finances tight, or someone emotionally unavailable—you didn't have the tools or perspective to realize that it wasn't your problem. So, you created a story: *If I can manage this, I'll be safe. If I can keep everyone happy, I'll be okay.*

What you must realize is it wasn't true then, and it's not true now. Life was never predictable, and trying to control every moving piece is like playing whack-a-mole with the universe. The moment you think you've got it all nailed down, something else pops up. Why? Because life is inherently unpredictable. Trillions of moving parts colliding in the present moment called the now. That's the deal. And trying to control it? That's just exhausting.

Let's get real for a second. High achievers love control. You thrive on plans, outcomes, and results. And hey, that's served you well—at least professionally. But the problem is that you've taken that same mindset and applied it to life. You think if you just work harder, think faster, or strategize better, you can bend reality to your will.

Spoiler alert: You can't.

Think about it—have you ever actually controlled everything? Even on your best day, did the world conform to your plans without a single hiccup? Of course not. And yet, you keep trying, as if one more to-do list or contingency plan will finally lock the universe into place.

It's absurd when you think about it. Control isn't just an illusion; it's a bad joke. Life is unpredictable, messy, and wildly out of your hands. The weather doesn't care about your picnic plans. Your toddler doesn't care about your meeting schedule. And the stock market sure as hell doesn't care about your retirement goals.

Here's the real tragedy of trying to control everything: it's robbing you of the peace you're so desperate to feel. You're so busy managing, fixing, and planning that you've left no room for joy, spontaneity, or connection.

Jessica's need for control wasn't just about keeping chaos at bay; it was about protecting herself from pain. But in trying to shield herself from uncertainty, she ended up building a prison of her own making—one where she was constantly exhausted, anxious, and disconnected.

Sound familiar? Maybe you've built your own prison, too. You've traded freedom for the illusion of safety, only to find that the walls you've built aren't keeping the chaos out—they're keeping you trapped inside.

Here's the part you don't want to hear, but desperately need to: the only thing you can control is you. That's it. Not your partner, not your kids, not your employees, not the outcome of that deal, and certainly not the universe.

What you can control is how you respond to life's unpredictability. You can control your perspective, your choices, and the meaning you assign to events. Everything else? That's out of your hands.

So why keep wasting your energy on things you can't control? It's like trying to rearrange deck chairs on the Titanic while the ship's going down. Your need for control isn't saving you—it's drowning you.

I know what you're thinking, "*if I let go of control, everything will fall apart*." But here's the irony, you don't actually have control now anyway. Letting go isn't about giving up; it's about acknowledging reality. It's about saying, "I can't control the storm, but I can decide how I'm going to weather it."

Yes, it's scary. Letting go feels like stepping into the unknown. But peace doesn't come from having everything under control, it comes from accepting that you don't need to.

The Role of Shame and Guilt

As our conversation deepened, Jessica began to recognize a feeling of guilt that she hadn't fully acknowledged before.

"Whenever I even think about letting go, I feel guilty," she admitted. "It's like, if I'm not doing everything, I'm being selfish or irresponsible."

"That's common, especially for high achievers," I said. "But here's the thing: control isn't the same as care. Letting go doesn't mean you care less—it means you're learning to trust more. The world won't crumble just because you take a step back."

Jessica listened closely, letting the words settle. "So, I can still care without carrying everything on my shoulders?"

"Yes," I affirmed. "And that's part of the lesson here. It's about learning to separate control from care."

You are not here to be everyone's hero. And guess what? You never were. Somewhere along the way, you confused care with control, thinking that if you don't keep everything running smoothly, it's somehow your fault if things fall apart. But **caring isn't the same as carrying**, and it's time to separate the two.

Think about it, who asked you to hold all this weight? Who told you it was your job to make sure everyone was okay? No one. Yet, here you are, carrying it all, out of some misguided sense of duty. It's time to set that down. Those responsibilities? They weren't yours then, and they aren't yours now.

Jessica realized she'd been living life as a balancing act, taking on too much because letting go felt terrifying.

"I've always felt that resting is lazy, and asking for help is a weakness," she admitted.

"High achievers often do," I replied. "But it's exhausting. The belief that you have to manage everything alone comes from a place rooted in childhood, not reality."

Jessica sighed, "It's like I've been running this race my whole life, trying to manage everything."

How This Might Be Showing Up in Your Life Today

Maybe you see a bit of yourself in Jessica's story, but let's get specific. How could this habit of taking on what was never yours to carry be playing out in your life right now?

- **At Work**: Are you the one who always says "yes," even when you're stretched thin? Do you find yourself taking on tasks outside your job description because you feel like it's up to you to keep everything from falling apart?
- **In Relationships**: Are you the "go-to" for everyone's problems, the one people turn to when they need a solution? Are you constantly trying to fix things for others, thinking that if they're okay, you'll be okay?
- **With Your Family**: Maybe you still feel the need to "keep the peace" in your family, trying to manage everyone's emotions and keep things running smoothly. Perhaps you're so busy trying to be the glue that you've forgotten how to just be yourself.

Whatever the situation, the message is the same: You've taken on responsibilities and roles that aren't yours, and it's exhausting you.

Boundaries as the Foundation of Peace

Jessica's struggle with boundaries was painfully familiar—not just to her, but to so many high achievers who feel the weight of being everything to everyone. She sighed as we delved deeper into the subject, already aware of how much saying "yes" all the time was costing her.

"Saying no feels like I'm failing someone," she confessed. "I feel like I have to be available for everyone, all the time."

I leaned forward and looked her in the eye. "Jessica, saying no isn't failing others. It's how you respect yourself. Boundaries aren't walls to shut people out—they're guardrails to protect your peace. Without boundaries, you're wide open to everyone else's demands, and that's a fast track to burnout and resentment."

Jessica nodded hesitantly. "I guess I've never thought of boundaries like that."

"Let me put it this way," I said. "Boundaries are how you create peace. They say, "This is my line. This is my space. This is how I protect my energy." Without boundaries, peace is impossible. And if you don't respect your own boundaries, how can you expect anyone else to?"

Boundaries are the ultimate act of self-respect. They tell the world, I value myself enough to protect my time, my energy, and my well-being. When you don't have boundaries, you send the opposite message, I don't value myself enough to say no.

If you don't respect yourself, how can you expect others to? People without boundaries are like unlocked doors—anyone can walk in, take what they want, and leave without a second thought. People don't respect what's freely given without limits. Boundaries force others to acknowledge your value because they make it clear that you won't tolerate anything less.

Here's the thing about boundaries—they're meaningless unless you enforce them. A boundary without consequences is just a suggestion, and let's be real, who takes suggestions seriously? If someone crosses your line and you let it slide, you're teaching them that your words mean nothing. Enforcing the consequences of a boundary is what makes it real.

Jessica struggled with this at first. "But doesn't enforcing boundaries make me seem like…you know…an asshole?" she asked hesitantly.

"Jessica, do you think people with boundaries have peace?" I asked.

She thought for a moment and nodded. "Yeah, I guess they do."

"Exactly," I said. "Because boundaries aren't about being an asshole—they're about protecting your peace. And yes, people without boundaries might label you as difficult, or even selfish, but you know what those so-called 'assholes' have? Peace. They're not running around trying to please everyone at their own expense. They're living their lives on their terms."

Jessica laughed nervously, "I guess I've been too scared of being seen as selfish."

"Here's the reality," I said. "The only people who will truly be upset about your boundaries are the ones who benefited from you not having any. If someone leaves your life because you set a boundary, they weren't there for you—they were there for what they could get away with."

Boundaries have a way of filtering out the people who don't belong in your life. When you set a boundary and someone reacts poorly—by guilt-tripping you, getting angry, or threatening to leave—that's not a sign you're doing something wrong. It's a sign that their relationship with you was conditional on you sacrificing your well-being for their benefit.

True relationships—whether friendships, family, or romantic—thrive when boundaries are in place because they're built on mutual respect. The people who truly care about you will honor your boundaries, even if it's inconvenient for them. They'll understand that your boundaries are how you show up as your best self—not just for you, but for them too.

"Jessica," I said, "you can't rest your body or your mind without boundaries. You can't protect your energy or focus on what matters most. Without boundaries, your life becomes a revolving door for other people's demands, leaving you exhausted and disconnected from yourself."

She nodded again, this time with more conviction. "So, boundaries are about giving myself permission to rest?"

"Exactly. Boundaries give you the space to breathe, to rest, and to actually live your life instead of just managing everyone else's. When you enforce your boundaries, you're telling yourself—and everyone else—that you're worth protecting."

Making Boundaries Work for You

The key to making boundaries work is to recognize that they're not just about saying no—they're about saying yes to the life you want to live. Every time you enforce a boundary, you're creating room for what truly matters: your peace, your passions, your health, and your joy.

"Jessica, think about it this way," I said. "Every time you let someone cross a boundary without consequences, you're giving away a piece of yourself. But every time you enforce a boundary, you're reclaiming your power. You're showing the world—and yourself—that you matter."

Now, let me bring this back to you. If you're reading this and feeling a little uncomfortable, good. That's the point. Because the truth is, boundaries are hard, especially if you've spent your whole life putting everyone else's needs above your own. But here's the reality: you can't pour from an empty cup, and you can't live a peaceful, fulfilling life without boundaries.

Ask yourself:

- Where in your life are you letting people cross your lines?
- What would it feel like to finally say no without guilt?
- How would your life change if you enforced your boundaries with confidence?

Boundaries aren't about being selfish—they're about being whole. They're how you protect your peace, your energy, and your sense of self. And yes, some people might not like it. But that's their problem, not yours.

Because at the end of the day, the people who truly belong in your life will respect your boundaries. And the ones who don't? Well, you don't need them anyway.

Jessica's Life After the Breakthrough

When Jessica finally understood this, she felt a weight lift off her shoulders. She realized she'd been living under the illusion that her worth was tied to how much she could manage. But once she let go, she discovered something she hadn't felt in years: **freedom**.

Imagine that for yourself. You're allowed to put down the weight you picked up years ago. You're allowed to rest– the world won't fall apart without you. Imagine the energy you'd save, the peace you'd feel, and the life you'd finally get to live.

Once Jessica embraced the truth that it wasn't her job to carry everyone else's burdens, her life changed. She no longer felt compelled to manage every detail. She set down the weight she'd carried for years, and for the first time, she felt truly free. Her health improved, her relationships deepened, and she discovered a peace she never thought possible.

Jessica now shows up for herself and others without feeling like she has to control everything. She's found a balance she never thought possible—one rooted in self-respect and the understanding that her worth isn't tied to how much she can fix.

A Shift That Sets You Free

Jessica's story might resonate with you, but this chapter isn't about her; it's about you. It's about recognizing that you are already whole, and that the roles and responsibilities you took on as a child were never yours to begin with. The truth is, the struggles you absorbed, the responsibilities you felt were yours to manage—they were never your business. They belonged to the adults in your life, and it's okay to let them go.

Imagine telling that younger version of yourself, *"You don't need to fix this. This isn't your job."* Feel the relief of that truth. Whatever weight you took on as a child—whether it was managing others' emotions, being the "peacekeeper," or trying to fix things you couldn't control—it wasn't yours to carry. It was never your fault, and it was never your job.

It's okay to let go, to let that child inside of you off the hook. You are allowed to rest, to ask for help, and to trust that things can be okay without you holding everything together. You did the best you could with what you knew. Now it's time to take a deep breath, release the weight, and step into the freedom and peace that's been waiting for you all along.

Reflective Questions

Take a moment to reflect:

- What responsibilities did you take on as a child that were never yours to carry?
- Where in your life are you still trying to control everything?
- What would it feel like to let go of some of that control?
- Who could you ask for help, and what's stopping you from asking?
- If you could release one responsibility right now that's weighing you down, what would it be?

Chapter 10

Key #4: Everyone Is Doing the Best They Can with the Mind and Resources They Have at the Time

Imagine being punished for getting the answers wrong on a test you didn't even know you were supposed to be taking, in a class you didn't know you were supposed to be in, at a university you didn't even know existed. Sounds absurd, right? But that's exactly what you're doing when you judge others—especially your parents—for failing to meet your expectations.

You tell yourself, *"They should've known better."* But the truth is, they didn't. People, including your parents, were making the best decisions they could with the mental tools, emotional intelligence, and resources they had at the time. And just because their best didn't meet your expectations, it doesn't mean they didn't care. It just means they were human.

Meet Michael

Michael had been a law enforcement officer for over 15 years, and to the outside world, he seemed like a hero. He was the guy who could handle anything—crisis situations, high-pressure moments, the worst of humanity. But what most people didn't see was the toll it was taking on him.

Michael had developed a deep mistrust of people. His job required him to deal with humanity on its worst days—domestic disputes, crimes of passion, and the aftermath of terrible decisions. Over time, this eroded his ability to see the good in anyone. And it wasn't just strangers—he carried that same mistrust into his personal life.

He had a drinking problem he wouldn't admit to himself. His relationships were strained, with walls so high that even the people closest to him couldn't get in. And at work, his colleagues whispered about how he was becoming bitter, closed off, and impossible to approach. But underneath all of this was a deeper pain, one he'd carried since he was a child.

As a boy, Michael grew up watching his father beat his mother. He was just 5 years old the first time he threw himself between them, screaming for his dad to stop. It didn't work. His father shoved him aside, and Michael was left trembling, helpless, and angry.

From that moment, Michael swore he'd never be powerless again. He developed a savior complex, a rigid sense of justice, and an unwillingness to forgive. His father became the villain in his mind—the man who taught him that the world was cruel and unfair, that people couldn't be trusted, and that he had to hold on to his anger to stay strong.

But as Michael shared his story with me, I asked him a question that shifted everything, "What if your dad was really doing the best he could with what he had at the time?"

Michael recoiled, anger flashing in his eyes. "What are you talking about? He was a monster. He destroyed my family. How could that be his best?"

I nodded. "I hear you. But let me ask you something. Do you know what your father's childhood was like? Do you know what tools he had, what pain he was carrying, or what he'd been taught about love, anger, and control?"

Michael paused. "Not really. He never talked about it."

"Maybe he didn't know any other way to be," I said gently. "What if the only tools he had were the only tools he had?"

Judgment: A Misunderstanding of Innocence

Let's talk about judgment, the mental sport most of us are Olympic-level athletes in. When we judge someone, it's almost never about what they've done. It's about our refusal to see their innocence. And no, I'm not talking about some courtroom kind of innocence. I'm talking about a deeper kind of innocence—the kind that says, "This person is doing the best they can **with the consciousness they have in this moment**."

But what do we do instead? We slap a label on them, roll our eyes, and make them the villain in the story we're writing in our heads. Why? Because it's easier than admitting that, maybe, just maybe, they're acting out of their own pain or ignorance. Or worse, it's easier than admitting that we've been just like them at some point.

When you judge someone else, you're not just making them guilty—you're making yourself guilty too. Judgment boomerangs back on you because deep down, you're denying innocence in them and, by extension, in yourself. It's like the universe has this unspoken rule, "If you can't see innocence in them, you can't see it in you either." And that's where guilt creeps in.

Let me break it down. When you look at someone's behavior and think, "*Ugh, how could they?*" what you're really saying is, "If I ever acted like that, I wouldn't forgive myself." You're holding them to a standard you can't meet because you're carrying guilt for your own past mistakes—mistakes you haven't forgiven yourself for because you didn't see your own innocence at the time.

You know what's really wild? We make fun of "gullible" people like it's some kind of sport. But think about what we're really saying, "*Haha, look at you, you still trust people. You haven't been traumatized enough to see the world as a dangerous, manipulative place like I do.*" How twisted is that? We're mocking their innocence, their ability to believe in the good in others, because it highlights how much of ours we've lost.

Why do gullible people get tricked? Because they don't see deviousness in others—they can't, because it doesn't exist in them. They operate from a place of trust, and instead of admiring that, we ridicule it. But here's some more hard truth: what we're actually laughing at is their lack of trauma. And if that's not a sign that we've got some healing to do, I don't know what is.

Judgment Is a Mirror

Let me bring this home with a story. My wife and I once had a fight—one of those long, drawn-out fights that creates tension for months. It all started because I felt like she didn't "have my back" in a situation with one of her friends. I grew up in an environment where loyalty meant everything, where you backed your people no matter what, even if it meant throwing hands. That's just how it was. So, when my wife didn't react the way I thought she should, I felt betrayed.

For almost a year, I carried this resentment, thinking, *"How can I trust someone who doesn't have my back?"* But then it hit me: my wife didn't grow up in the kind of environment I did. She wasn't raised in a war zone where every day was a battle for survival. She grew up in love, not trauma. Her world wasn't built on "us versus them." She still had her innocence, and I was mad at her for it.

I realized I was holding her to a standard built from my own trauma. I was judging her for not being emotionally damaged in the same way I was. Think about how insane that is—I was punishing her for her peace. That's when I had to let go of my judgment. I had to see her innocence and, in doing so, recognize the ways I'd lost my own.

Judgment always tells you more about yourself than it does about the other person. When you judge someone, you're projecting your own unhealed wounds onto them. It's like holding up a mirror and saying, "I don't like what I see in you because it reminds me of something I can't face in me."

Take my wife, for example. My judgment of her was really a reflection of how I hadn't dealt with my own issues. It wasn't her that needed to change—it was me. The same is true for you. Every time someone triggers you, it's an opportunity to ask, "What unhealed part of me is this reflecting back?"

On a deeper, more spiritual level, judgment creates separation. It puts you on one side and the person you're judging on the other. And separation is the opposite of peace. Peace is about unity, about recognizing the oneness of all things. Judgment says, "I'm better than you," or sometimes, "You're better than me." Either way, it's a divide. And as long as you live in that divide, peace will always feel just out of reach.

When Jesus told Peter to forgive 77 x 7 times, he wasn't just throwing out random math for fun. He was pointing to a deeper truth: forgiveness isn't a one-and-done deal. It is a limitless practice, a daily (sometimes hourly) choice to let go of the judgment and resentment that keep you tied to the past.

Jesus also said, "Judge not, that you be not judged." It's not because God's up there keeping score, ready to zap you for being judgmental. It's because judgment is a mirror. The judgments you hold against others are the ones you secretly hold against yourself. When you stop judging others, you free yourself from the guilt and shame that come from holding yourself to impossible standards. That's where the peace comes in.

The Perspective Shift

As we dug deeper, Michael began to see the patterns. His father had grown up in a violent household himself, where hitting was the way problems were solved and emotions weren't talked about. His father didn't have the emotional tools to do better because no one had ever shown him a different way.

This didn't excuse his father's behavior, but it helped Michael see it for what it was—a reflection of his father's pain and limitations, not a reflection of Michael's worth.

"That doesn't make it okay," Michael said, his voice tight.

"No, it doesn't," I agreed. "But it also means it wasn't about you. Your dad's actions weren't a test of your value or measure as a man—they were a reflection of his own struggles, his own pain, and his own feelings of brokenness. Whether you want to accept it or not, he was doing the best he could with what he had, even if his best was awful."

For Michael, this realization was like cracking open a door that had been locked for years.

How This Ties to You

Let's get something straight, people aren't their actions. Their actions are a reflection of their level of consciousness in that moment. And guess what? The same goes for you. Every mistake you've ever made wasn't because you were evil or broken—it was because you didn't know a better way emotionally. Maybe you knew better intellectually, but until you understand it emotionally, you're not capable of choosing differently.

This is why judgment is so pointless. When you judge someone for their actions, you're ignoring the fact that they're acting from the best awareness they have at the time. If they knew better, they'd do better. And if you knew better in your past, you would've done better too. Read the previous sentence over and over again until you truly understand. It's not enough to understand this logically—you've got to feel it in your bones.

Michael's story might seem specific, but the lesson is universal. Whether it's your parents, a boss, a partner, or anyone else who's hurt you, the truth is this: People are doing the best they can with the mind and resources they have at the time.

That doesn't mean their actions are excusable. It doesn't mean you have to like them or let them back into your life. But it does mean that their behavior was never about you.

Maybe your mom wasn't emotionally available because she was carrying her own unhealed wounds. Maybe your dad wasn't there for you because he was trying to survive his own demons. Maybe the person who hurt you was acting from their own feelings of brokenness, not from any truth about your value.

When you stop taking it personally and start seeing their actions as a reflection of where *they* were—not who *you* are—you free yourself from the chains of resentment and anger. Again, picture your child coming to you later in life saying what you did or didn't say or do to them screwed them up somehow. What would you say? I bet it would be something along the lines of "I did the best I could. I was dealing with so much at the time when you were too young to understand." And yet you won't extend that same grace to those who hurt you in the past? Is that not the very definition of a hypocrite?

Holding on to anger, mistrust, and resentment might feel like control, but it's a trap. It's like carrying a burning coal in your hand and then throwing it at the person who wronged you, hoping it'll hurt them, except they'll just duck leaving you with a burned hand.

Michael spent years carrying his anger toward his father, and it bled into every area of his life. It made him hard, distant, and mistrustful. It drove him to drink, pushed people away, and left him feeling isolated and empty.

But when he started to see his father's actions for what they truly were—not a reflection of Michael's worth, but of his father's pain and limitations—he began to let go. And with that letting go came peace.

Now, let's imagine for a second what would happen if you let all that go. No judgment. No grudges. Just… peace.

When you let go of judgment, you stop resisting what is. That resistance—telling yourself this shouldn't have happened or they shouldn't have done that—is what creates your suffering. Letting go doesn't mean you're saying what happened was okay; it means you're saying, "I refuse to let this control me anymore."

Think about Jesus for a moment. Here was a man who was betrayed, beaten, and crucified. If anyone had a reason to hold a grudge, it was him. But what did he say? "Father, forgive them, for they know not what they do." That wasn't weakness—that was power. He understood that the people who hurt him were acting from their own pain, their own ignorance. He saw their innocence, even when they couldn't see it themselves.

Jesus wasn't just talking about them, though. He was modeling something for us. He was showing us that forgiveness is how you transcend suffering. It's how you let go of the chains of judgment and step into the freedom of peace.

When you let go of judgment, something magical happens. Your inner world starts to reflect your outer world. The people and situations that used to trigger you don't feel so heavy anymore. That coworker who always gets under your skin? Suddenly, you see their struggle instead of their attitude. That family member who let you down? You start to understand that they were doing the best they could.

And the best part? When you let go of judgment for others, you naturally start letting it go for yourself. You stop replaying the highlight reel of your mistakes and start seeing your own innocence. That's the ultimate gift of forgiveness: not just freedom for others, but freedom for yourself.

Forgiveness: The Antidote to Judgment

Here's the thing about judgment, it's a trap and it's exhausting. It makes you feel superior for a moment, but it locks you into guilt and disconnects you from your own innocence. Carrying around the weight of what someone should've done or how they should've acted is like walking through life dragging a bag of bricks you packed yourself. Every judgment you make is another brick in that bag, and the only person it weighs down is you.

So, what's the answer? Forgiveness. Not the weak, passive kind that says, "It's okay, I'll let it slide." Real forgiveness is about recognizing the innocence in others—and in yourself. It's about seeing that everyone, no matter how messy their behavior, is doing the best they can with the level of consciousness they have at the moment.

When you forgive, you're not letting someone off the hook or excusing their behavior. You're just letting yourself off the hook from carrying around judgment, guilt, and resentment. Forgiveness isn't about them—it's about freeing yourself. It's about saying, "I see your humanity, and in doing so, I reclaim mine."

That recognition—that we're all doing the best we can with the consciousness we have in the moment—is what bridges the gap between us. And in that connection, there's peace.

Spiritually, when you let go of judgment, you stop resisting the flow of life. Judgment is a wall, but forgiveness is a doorway. It lets light in. It lets love in. And it lets peace in. Judgment locks you in a prison of your own making. Forgiveness is the key to breaking free.

It's how you stop punishing yourself and others for not knowing better. And when you can see the innocence in others, you'll start to see it in yourself. That's where real peace begins.

Bringing It Home

Everyone is doing the best they can with the mind and resources they have at the time. That includes the people who hurt you. That includes your parents. And yes, that includes *you*.

This isn't about excusing bad behavior. It's about understanding that people's actions come from their own struggles, not from anything you did or didn't do.

Michael didn't forgive his father overnight, and you don't have to rush your process either. But consider this, what if the person who hurt you wasn't trying to break you? What if they were just trying to survive their own pain? What if instead of holding on to the emotions for protection, you allowed the wisdom learned from the encounter to protect you? What is the point of holding the anger or resentment if you're the only one being hurt by it? That's like hitting yourself in the head with a brick to give the person you resent a headache, isn't it?

When you see their actions for what they are—a reflection of them, not you—you set yourself free.

And isn't that what you deserve? Peace. Freedom. The ability to move forward without the weight of someone else's issues holding you back.

The time to let go is now. Not for them, but for you.

My invitation to you is to let go of the judgment you're holding on to. Just for today, try it. When you feel the urge to judge, pause. Ask yourself, "What part of their innocence am I refusing to see? What part of mine?" And then let it go. Not because they deserve it, but because you deserve the peace that comes with it. As Jesus said, forgive 77 x 7—not for their sake, but for yours. Peace is waiting. The question is, are you ready to claim it?

Michael's Life After the Breakthrough

After confronting his deeply ingrained judgments and his unwillingness to forgive, Michael began to experience life in a way he never thought possible. Michael realized that his father's actions, though hurtful and damaging, were not personal attacks on him but reflections of a man battling his own pain and limitations. He no longer saw his father as a villain but as a deeply flawed human being doing the best he could with the broken tools he had. A man that needed to be shown more love, not more judgment.

This shift in perspective rippled into every aspect of Michael's life. At work, he began to see the people he dealt with not as "the worst of humanity" but as individuals caught in moments of pain, fear, or desperation. This newfound compassion softened his hardened exterior, making him a better officer, colleague, and leader. His interactions became less about control and judgment and more about understanding and de-escalating.

In his personal life, Michael started to dismantle the walls he had built. His relationships improved as he let go of the need to protect himself from imagined betrayals. He repaired friendships that had fallen apart and found deeper intimacy with his partner. Most importantly, he stopped numbing his pain with alcohol. By addressing the root of his anger and mistrust, he no longer needed the bottle to escape.

The most significant breakthrough for Michael was the realization that forgiveness wasn't about letting others off the hook; it was about releasing himself from the chains of judgment and resentment. In forgiving his father, he forgave himself for the years he spent carrying that anger. And in that act of forgiveness, he found a peace he hadn't known since childhood. For the first time in years, Michael felt light, free, and at peace.

A Shift That Sets You Free

Freedom begins with a decision—a decision to see things differently, to let go of the stories that have held you captive, and to reclaim your power from the grip of judgment and resentment. Forgiveness is about liberating yourself from the invisible chains that tie you to the past.

For Michael, the shift came when he stopped asking, *"Why did this happen to me?"* and started asking, *"What was happening in them?"* This simple but profound change in perspective allowed him to see his father not as a monster, but as a man struggling under the weight of his own pain. It not only erased the hurt; it rewrote the narrative.

This shift is available to you, too. When you release the need to make others wrong or to carry the burden of their actions, you create space for peace to enter your life. You're no longer tethered to the emotions and judgments that keep you stuck. Instead, you step into a state of clarity and compassion—not just for others, but for yourself.

When you forgive, you don't lose control—you gain it. Real control doesn't come from holding grudges or staying angry; it comes from choosing how you respond. It's about taking ownership of your emotional state and deciding that your peace is more important than reliving old wounds.

Think of forgiveness as putting down a heavy backpack you've carried for years. Each grudge, judgment, and resentment is a rock in that bag, weighing you down. The more you hold on to it, the harder it is to move forward. But when you forgive, you set the bag down. You feel lighter. Freer. You stop carrying weight that was never yours to bear.

This isn't about letting people off the hook or pretending the hurt didn't happen. It's about recognizing that their actions were about them—not you—and deciding that you're no longer willing to let their feelings of brokenness break you.

Imagine what your life could look like if you let go. What could you achieve if your energy wasn't tied up in anger and judgment? Who could you become if you stopped replaying the past and started creating your future? Forgiveness is the key to that door. And once you walk through it, you'll wonder why you ever waited so long.

Reflective Questions

Take a moment to reflect:

- What judgments are you holding onto, and how are they impacting your peace of mind?
- Who in your life do you struggle to forgive, and what story are you telling yourself about their actions?
- What part of your own innocence are you denying when you judge others?
- What beliefs about forgiveness are holding you back?
- How might letting go of judgment improve your relationships?
- What is one step you can take today to release a grudge or judgment?

Chapter 11

Key #5: You Were Loved, Just Not the Way You Wanted to Be Loved

As children, we experience the world through the lens of our needs. When we feel love, we feel safe, seen, and valued. But when the love we receive doesn't align with what we want or think we need, it's easy to believe it isn't love at all. We start telling ourselves stories—stories of neglect, rejection, or unworthiness—that often carry into adulthood.

The truth is, there's a difference between not being loved and not being loved the way *you* wanted. The gap between those two realities is where most of our pain comes from. It's in that gap that we start to misunderstand the intentions of the people who raised us, misinterpreting their actions—or lack of actions—as evidence that we weren't loved at all.

What if the love you didn't feel as a child was there all along, just in a form you couldn't recognize? What if your parents were loving you the only way they knew how, shaped by their own experiences and limitations?

This chapter is about bridging that gap—about seeing the love that may have been present but hidden beneath the surface. It's about understanding that just because love wasn't expressed in the way you needed doesn't mean it wasn't there. And it's about finding peace with the love you did receive, even if it didn't come wrapped in the package you hoped for.

Meet Dr. Debra

Dr. Debra is a highly respected school principal. Fierce, accomplished, and determined. But beneath her polished exterior, Debra was lonely. In her 50s, she found herself longing for connection, love, and vulnerability—things she had never learned to give or receive. And like so many of us, her story started with a misunderstanding about the love she thought she didn't get.

Dr. Debra was the kind of woman who commanded attention. As the principal of a high-performing charter school, she was known for her no-nonsense approach. Teachers either rose to her standards or quickly found themselves looking for new jobs. Her students respected her, but they also feared her.

Her personal life, however, was a different story. Dr. Debra had been single for over a decade, and her dating life was a series of short-lived relationships that always ended the same way. "Men just can't handle a strong woman," she would say dismissively. But beneath that bravado was a woman who was deeply afraid—afraid of being vulnerable, afraid of being rejected, and ultimately, afraid of being unloved.

When Dr. Debra came to me, she admitted she didn't want to spend the rest of her life alone. "I don't want to die lonely, Elijah," she said, her voice breaking for the first time during our session. "But I don't know how to let anyone in. Every time I try, I just end up pushing them away."

I asked her to tell me about her childhood. "What was it like growing up with your mom?" I asked.

Dr. Debra sighed. "Strict. That's the only word I can use to describe it. My mom was tough. There were no hugs, no 'I love you,' no softness. She was always correcting me, always finding something I was doing wrong. It felt like nothing I did was ever good enough."

"And what did little Debra make that mean?" I asked gently.

"That she was unloved," she said without hesitation. "I felt like I didn't matter to her, like I wasn't worth her time or affection."

I leaned in. "Tell me more," I said. "What did she do, or didn't do, that made you feel she didn't love you?"

Dr. Debra paused for a moment. "She never said she loved me. Never hugged me. She was always so hard on me. Everything was about discipline and rules. It was like… I don't know… like she was preparing me for war or something."

"Let me ask you something," I said. "What do you know about your mom's life before she had you?"

Dr. Debra's brow furrowed. "I know she grew up in the segregated South. She had a tough life, working on farms and raising her siblings. But we never really talked about it."

"Let's talk about that for a second," I said. "What do you think life was like for a young Black woman growing up in the segregated South?"

Dr. Debra's expression softened. "I know it wasn't easy."

"Not easy is putting it mildly," I said. "Your mom grew up in a time when the color of her skin dictated every aspect of her life. She couldn't walk into certain stores, drink from certain water fountains, or even look a white person in the eye without risking her safety. She lived in a world that told her, every single day, that she was less than. And as a Black woman, she didn't just have to deal with racism—she also had to navigate the expectations and limitations placed on her as a woman. That's double the weight to carry."

I could see Dr. Debra processing this, so I continued. "Think about this, in that era survival wasn't just about living day to day. It was about avoiding humiliation, physical harm, or even death. Your mother couldn't afford to trust easily. She had to be strong, self-reliant, and guarded. Every interaction with the outside world was a potential threat."

Dr. Debra's eyes widened as this reality started to sink in.

"For Black women during Jim Crow," I explained, "life wasn't just about personal struggles. It was about holding up entire families and communities in a world designed to tear them down. Your mom probably watched her own mother or aunts endure backbreaking work as maids, cooks, or sharecroppers, often for pennies. She saw them swallow their pride to keep food on the table. And if they showed too much softness, too much vulnerability, they risked being seen as weak—and weakness in that world could be deadly."

Dr. Debra looked down, her mind clearly turning over these truths.

"Now imagine this," I continued. "Your mom grows up in that environment, and then she has you. She's carrying all that pain, all that survival instinct, all those walls she had to build to protect herself.

"Do you have children?" I asked.

"Yes. I have two," she responded.

"And as a parent, what is your number one job?" I said.

"To protect them," she replied.

"Protect them from what?" I whispered softly.

"The world?" She said quickly looking a bit confused.

"No, " I replied, "You don't know the whole world."

Suddenly her eyes widened and she shouted, "I am protecting them from my world. The hurts and challenges that I experienced!"

"Now you're getting it," I said. "And the same was true for your mom. In her mind, the best way to love you—the best way to prepare you for a world she knew would be just as harsh—was to make you tough. Because to her, toughness was love. Toughness was survival."

Dr. Debra's eyes welled up. "She thought she was protecting me?"

"Yes," I said. "Your mom didn't grow up in a world that rewarded vulnerability or softness. She thought, "If I can make you strong, then no one will hurt you the way the world hurt me." Her love was tough because her life was tough from her perspective. But it was love, Doc. It was the only way she knew how to love. It just wasn't the love you wanted."

Dr. Debra sat silently for a moment, her tears spilling over. "I thought… I thought she didn't care."

"She cared deeply," I said. "She just didn't know how to show it in the way you needed. But that doesn't mean it wasn't love."

Dr. Debra's mom wasn't withholding affection to hurt her. She was loving her the only way she knew how—through preparation and protection. She didn't say, "I love you," because in her world, words weren't enough. Actions were what mattered.

The truth is, your parents didn't raise you for the environment you grew up in—they raised you for the environment *they* grew up in. They tried to protect you from their trauma, often by passing it down to you and calling it protection. In their minds, they were shielding you from what they experienced, even though those experiences may not match the reality you're living in today.

I once had a client whose mother never let her attend sleepovers. The client saw it as controlling and unfair, but when we dug deeper, we uncovered the truth: the mother had been molested during a family sleepover as a child. In her mind, forbidding her daughter from going to sleepovers wasn't about punishment—it was about protection. This is how trauma gets passed down. Parents unintentionally hand us their fears in the name of love.

But this isn't just about understanding their world—it's also about understanding how we see our parents. Most people are still viewing them through the eyes of the child they once were, not the adult they've become. And that perspective shapes how they interpret everything their parents did or didn't do.

A Prisoner's Realization

Let me tell you about a man I worked with in prison, serving a 20-year sentence for murder. When we started talking about this topic of being loved, but not in the way we wanted, he became visibly angry. "How could putting me up for adoption be considered love?" he asked. "I never even met my birth mother. She gave me away like I was nothing."

I could see he was still looking at his mother through the eyes of the child he'd been, the one who felt abandoned and unloved. So, I challenged him to see her through an adult's perspective instead.

I asked, "Do you have any idea what it takes for a mother to give up her child, especially right after giving birth? Let me share something personal. I was in the delivery room when my daughter was born. Even while she was still in the womb, I could see the connection between my wife and her. My wife could feel everything—every kick, every flutter. They were deeply connected before my daughter even took her first breath.

"Now imagine carrying a baby for nine months, feeling them grow inside you, and then going through the pain of childbirth, only to watch someone take that child out of the room, knowing you'll never see them again. Can you fathom what has to go through a woman's mind to make that choice?"

His expression began to soften as I continued.

"Think about what she must have believed about herself to make that decision. She likely thought she was so screwed up, so incapable, or so dangerous to you that you'd be better off with a stranger. Maybe she didn't have the emotional capacity to raise a child. Maybe she was strung out on drugs. Or maybe she'd been through so much trauma that she felt the only way to protect you was to let you go.

"Yes, foster care was hard for you. Yes, the environment you grew up in was brutal. But she couldn't have known how tough it would be for you. The only thing she knew was that she believed she wasn't good enough, and giving you up felt like the only way to give you a chance. That, my friend, is an excruciating decision. That's not a lack of love—it's the highest form of love she could offer at the time."

His eyes widened as the realization sank in. "Damn," he said quietly. "I got kids. It would be really hard to give them up."

"Exactly," I said. "That's how deep her love had to be. But you couldn't see that because you've been viewing her through a child's eyes. And that anger? It led you to commit a crime based on the emotions of an abandoned child. But now, this grown man you are today is serving the consequences."

He put his head down, shaking it slowly. "Damn," he whispered. "I had a chance to meet my mom once, and I didn't because I was too angry."

I nodded. "That's because you were still seeing her through the pain of that child. But what if you could see her through the eyes of the man you are now? What if you could understand that her choice wasn't about rejecting you—it was about loving you the only way she knew how?"

This shift in perspective isn't just for people in prison. It's for all of us. Many of us are walking through life holding on to anger, pain, and resentment toward our parents because we're still viewing them through the limited understanding of a child.

A child sees things in black and white, "If they loved me, they wouldn't have hurt me." But as adults, we gain the capacity to see the gray areas, to understand that love is complicated, messy, and sometimes painful.

What if you could see your parents through the lens of an adult? That doesn't mean excusing their mistakes or pretending the pain didn't happen. But it does mean releasing the idea that their choices define your worth. It means acknowledging that they were human, with their own wounds and limitations, navigating a world you didn't live in and making choices they thought were right.

So, the question isn't, "Did they love me the way I wanted?" it's, "Can I see the love they gave me for what it was, not what I wished it had been?"

New Age Parenting vs. The Reality of Generations Past

It's easy to sit here today, scrolling through self-help Instagram posts, binging YouTube videos about emotional intelligence, and taking online courses on parenting, and then turn around and think, *why didn't my parents do this?* But let me hit you with some context: *they couldn't.* They didn't have access to any of the stuff we do now. In fact, most of the things you think are "common sense" today didn't even exist as ideas when your parents were raising you.

Let's start with therapy. Today, it's practically a rite of passage. You can't throw a rock without hitting a podcast host, life coach, or someone who just finished their third round of couple's therapy. But for Baby Boomers and Gen X? Therapy wasn't just uncommon—it was taboo. Sigmund Freud, the so-called "father of psychology," introduced the idea of talking about your feelings over 100 years ago, and people laughed at him. Laughed. As in, "Why would anyone waste time talking about emotions? Just get over it."

Therapy was something you whispered about, not something you openly embraced.

Now, fast-forward to today. The personal development industry is a *$40 billion-a-year* behemoth. Yes, *billion*. And it's growing every single year. But do you know when all this started to take off? The 1980s. That's when people like Werner Erhard made personal development mainstream with programs like EST (Erhard Seminars Training now called "Landmark"). Before that? This whole idea of "inner work" was about as popular as kale smoothies in the 1960s—basically non-existent.

The reason *you* know about personal development is because it's been marketed to you for decades. You grew up in an era where self-help books are bestsellers, where Oprah is a cultural icon, and where anyone with an internet connection can Google their childhood trauma. But your parents? They were lucky if they stumbled across *Dear Abby* in the Sunday paper.

Let's Talk About Love—Old School Style

Now, let's talk about how love was expressed back in the day. Today, we've got entire shelves in bookstores dedicated to "love languages" (thanks, Gary Chapman). But back then? The only "language" your parents were fluent in was survival.

For them, love wasn't hugs and kisses and sitting down for heart-to-heart talks. Love was *practical*. It was putting food on the table, keeping a roof over your head, and making sure you didn't die of polio. Feelings? That was "New Age nonsense." You think your dad was going to sit you down and say, "Son, let's talk about how your emotions are impacting your self-esteem"? Not a chance. Love looked like working three jobs, coming home exhausted, and hoping you knew they cared because the lights were still on.

And now? You want to retroactively hold them accountable for not knowing about emotional intelligence when *Daniel Goleman* didn't even write the book on it until 1995? Come on. That's like blaming them for not using GPS when they grew up with paper maps. It's not just unfair—it's ridiculous.

We've only had access to all this personal development stuff for maybe 30 years, and most of us are still screwing it up. Be honest—how many times have you read a self-help book, nodded along, and then completely ignored it when it came time to put it into practice? How many of us are still going to therapy for the same issues we've been working on for years? We've got all the resources at our fingertips, and we're still fumbling the ball. And yet, we have the audacity to blame our parents for not knowing something that wasn't even *invented* when they were raising us?

Imagine you're at a fancy restaurant, eating a gourmet meal. You look over at someone eating canned beans in 1965, and you're like, "Wow, why aren't you eating filet mignon?" Uh, because it wasn't available to them! Honestly, you wouldn't even know about filet mignon if someone hadn't told you about it. The same goes for self-awareness, emotional intelligence, and parenting seminars. These things didn't just magically appear—they were built on decades of research, trial, and error. And the only reason you're even in a position to judge your parents is because *you were born into a time when this information is widely available.*

Here's a reality check, if self-development hadn't become trendy, you probably wouldn't be reading this book right now. You wouldn't even know to think about your childhood, much less blame your parents for not giving you the emotional support you wanted. And if you're feeling personally attacked right now, good. That means this is hitting where it needs to.

Your parents weren't working with podcasts, YouTube videos, or TikToks explaining trauma bonding and inner child work. They were working with what *they* were taught, which was probably, "Don't cry, or I'll give you something to cry about." That wasn't love to you—but to them, it was discipline. It was survival. It was the best they knew how to do.

So, before you get on your high horse about how they should've been more emotionally available, ask yourself this, *"Would you know any better if you were in their shoes?"* Be honest. If you didn't have access to every therapist, coach, and motivational speaker under the sun, would you magically know how to raise emotionally intelligent kids? Or would you be doing the same thing they did—just trying to survive?

Instead of blaming your parents for what they didn't know, maybe it's time to thank them for what they did. They loved you the only way they knew how. They did the best they could with what they had. And if you're sitting here reading this book, it means they got you this far. It means they did *enough*.

The truth is, blaming them for not meeting today's standards is like yelling at someone for not using emojis in a letter they wrote in 1973. It's absurd. So, let's stop pretending they had access to tools they didn't, and start appreciating that they did the best they could with what they had. And if you're ready to do better for the next generation? Great. But don't forget— you only know better because someone finally taught you.

My Father's Story

Let me share something personal. As I've shared in my first book and many of my talks, my own father struggled to show love the way I wanted him to. But it wasn't because he didn't care—it was because he never experienced love himself. When I asked him about his childhood, he told me something that stuck with me, "I knew nothing about love growing up. My mother never told me she loved me. In fact, we were given up for adoption as kids. And when I found her years later, she told me, 'I didn't want you then, and I don't want you now.'"

Imagine that. The person who was supposed to love him the most rejected him—*twice*. How do you bounce back from that? And then, a decade later, he had me. How could I expect him to know how to connect with me emotionally when he had no blueprint for what love even looked like? He wasn't withholding love out of malice—he simply didn't know how to give what he never received.

I carried so much resentment toward my dad for years. In my eyes, he was supposed to be my superhero, the one who made me feel safe, loved, and important. But he fell short of that, and it left me bitter. I judged him for everything he wasn't, everything he didn't do, and everything I thought he should've been.

But one day, I realized I was seeing him through the wrong lens. I wasn't looking at him as a human being with his own wounds, his own pain, and his own story. I was looking at him as a failed superhero. And that was the problem—he was never supposed to be a superhero. He was just a man, trying to figure out his own mess while raising a kid at the same time.

That was my hard pill to swallow. My dad didn't need my judgment—he needed my love. He needed someone to see him, not as a list of failures, but as a human being who had done the best he could with the tools he had. And once I understood that, everything started to shift.

I made a decision. I promised myself that I would love my dad in a way he'd never been loved. I would teach him what love looked like because no one had ever done that for him. Instead of waiting for him to figure it out, I decided to show him.

I stopped holding him to an impossible standard and started meeting him where he was. I called him. I told him I loved him. I asked him about his day, his life, his thoughts—things I'd never taken the time to do before. And slowly, something amazing happened.

Today, my dad and I are closer than ever. He calls to check on me all the time. He texts me just to say he loves me. But that wasn't who he was before. That's who he became because I showed him how. I didn't expect him to magically overcome decades of rejection and pain the moment I was born. Instead, I stepped into the role of teacher, and in doing so, I created the relationship I always wanted.

The Truth About Parenting

Here's something we don't talk about enough, parents don't automatically overcome their own issues just because they have kids. They don't suddenly shed all their pain, trauma, and bad habits the moment you're born. They're still figuring it out—just like you are now.

Think about your own life. Have you resolved every issue, healed every wound, and mastered every lesson? Probably not. Now imagine trying to do that while raising a child, paying bills, and navigating the ups and downs of life. That's what your parents were up against. They weren't superheroes. They were human beings, just trying to do the best they could with what they had.

This isn't about excusing their mistakes—it's about understanding them. It's about recognizing that their shortcomings weren't about you. They were about their own struggles, their own limitations, and their own unhealed wounds. And maybe, just maybe, it's your job now to help teach them what **unconditional** love looks like.

When I stopped expecting my dad to be someone he couldn't be and started seeing him for who he really was, I found peace. I realized that holding onto resentment wasn't just unfair—it was unproductive. It wasn't going to change him, and it sure as hell wasn't going to help me. But loving him? Meeting him where he was? That changed *everything*.

You have the power to rewrite the story. You can decide to stop judging your parents for what they didn't know and start teaching them what they didn't learn. You can be the one who shows them what love looks like. It won't be easy, but trust me, it's worth it. Because when you stop waiting for them to be something they're not and start loving them for who they are, you create a space for healing—for both of you.

This isn't just about your parents, though. It's about you. It's about recognizing that, just like your parents, you're doing the best you can with what you have. And when you see them with that same compassion, you free yourself from the burden of resentment and open the door to a relationship you never thought was possible.

Dr. Debra's Life After the Breakthrough

When Dr. Debra first came to me, she was the epitome of a successful leader: sharp, driven, and uncompromising. But beneath her professional armor, she was tired, lonely, and longing for a deeper connection. Her relationships, both romantic and personal, suffered because she didn't know how to open up or let her guard down. She thought vulnerability was a weakness and brushed off failed relationships with a sassy, "They just weren't strong enough to handle me." But the truth was, Dr. Debra didn't believe she deserved love.

Her journey to emotional freedom didn't happen overnight, but the transformation was undeniable. She began by seeing her mother in a new light—not as a harsh critic, but as a woman who loved fiercely in the only way she knew how. Understanding her mother's sacrifices and limitations allowed Dr. Debra to release decades of resentment and anger. And in doing so, she softened. She became kinder—not just to others, but to herself.

Today, Dr. Debra is in a loving, committed relationship with a partner who cherishes her for the strong yet vulnerable woman she's become. She no longer emasculates the men in her life; instead, she creates space for her partner to be his full self. Dr. Debra's ability to open her heart and let down her walls has allowed her to experience love in a way she never thought possible.

In her professional life, she's become an even better leader. Her newfound compassion has transformed the way she interacts with her team. Instead of micromanaging and controlling, she empowers those around her to grow and thrive. Her school has flourished under her leadership—not because she's less demanding, but because she now leads from a place of understanding and connection rather than fear and control.

Reframing Love

You want to know the truth about love? It doesn't always look the way you think it should. Love isn't just soft words, warm hugs, or grand gestures. Sometimes, love is hard. Sometimes, it's messy. And sometimes, it's so quiet that you miss it entirely.

Your parents loved you. They may not have loved you the way you wanted to be loved, but they loved you in the only way they knew how. And maybe that love came with limitations and pain, but it doesn't mean it wasn't real.

Reframing love means recognizing that it isn't about what someone gives you—it's about what you choose to see. Love is often hidden beneath layers of fear, pain, and survival. It's not always perfect, but it's always there if you're willing to look for it.

If you're holding on to resentment, judgment, or anger because you feel like you weren't loved the way you deserved, I want you to ask yourself: What is it costing you?

Holding on to the belief that you weren't loved doesn't just hurt your relationships—it hurts your peace. It creates a narrative that you're incomplete, unworthy, or somehow broken. You were never broken. You were never missing anything.

Understanding that you were loved—even imperfectly—allows you to let go of the stories that have kept you stuck. It frees you from the need to seek validation or approval from others. And when you release those chains, you step into the truth of who you really are: **already whole, already enough, already love.**

You don't need love from anyone because you *are* love.

When you strip away the resentment, the judgment, and the pain, what's left is your true self. And your true self is love. The kind of love that simply is.

You were born whole. You were born love. The problem is, you've spent years covering that truth with stories about why you're not enough—stories that someone else's actions wrote for you. But those stories aren't true. They never were.

When you let go of those stories—when you forgive, when you release judgment, when you see others and yourself through the lens of compassion—you step back into your wholeness. You realize there was nothing missing all along.

When you understand that you are already love, something amazing happens. You stop needing it. And when you stop needing love, you start giving it freely.

This doesn't mean you'll never experience hurt or disappointment. It means those experiences won't define you. They won't rob you of your peace or your joy. Because when you live from a place of love, you're unshakable.

Love becomes your way of being, not something you're searching for. And the more you give, the more you realize there's an endless supply—because it's who you are.

The Shift That Sets You Free

If you've been searching for emotional freedom and peace, this is the truth you need to embody. **You are already whole. You are already love.**

The pain you've been carrying—the anger, the resentment, the feeling of being unloved or unworthy—is not a reflection of who you are. It's a reflection of the stories you've believed. And those stories can change.

When you embrace these truths, everything shifts. You see your parents not as villains, but as human beings. You see yourself not as incomplete, but as whole. And you see love not as something to be earned, but as something you've always had.

I invite you to let go of the stories that have kept you from your peace. Accept the love that's always been there, even if it didn't come in the package you wanted. And live from the truth of who you really are.

Because when you do, you'll discover what Dr. Debra did: that the love you've been searching for was never outside of you. It was always within.

Reflective Questions

Take a moment to reflect:

- How did your parents' experiences shape the way they showed love to you?
- What stories have you been telling yourself about the way you were loved or not loved?
- In what ways have your expectations about love impacted your relationships and the way you show love to others?
- How would your life change if you stopped seeing love as something you need and started recognizing it as something you already are?
- What steps can you take to let go of resentment or judgment toward your parents or others who didn't love you the way you wanted?

Chapter 12

Key #6: All Human Behavior Is Motivated by Positive Intent (Just Not for Everyone Involved)

This might be one of the hardest things you'll ever hear, and I don't expect you to accept it all at once. Honestly, it's a bitter pill to swallow, especially when you think about the deep betrayals, the hurts, the unspeakable violations some of us have endured. To even entertain the idea that someone's harmful actions could have been motivated by a positive intent feels counterintuitive—if not downright offensive. But stay with me for a moment.

This isn't about excusing what they did. It's not about condoning harm, minimizing your pain, or saying you should "just get over it." Not at all. Your pain matters. What happened to you matters. But if we stop there, we stay in a place of suffering, holding onto the weight of what happened. And that's not where freedom lives.

What if I told you that understanding why people do what they do—why they hurt others, why they make selfish choices—has nothing to do with letting them off the hook and everything to do with setting yourself free?

You see, positive intent doesn't mean the action was good or justified. It means that, in the mind of the person doing the harm—whether they were fully aware of it or not—they believed their behavior was serving a need. Not for the person the harm was being done to. But for themselves.

The Six Basic Emotional Needs

All human behavior—whether healthy or destructive—comes down to meeting these six basic emotional needs (which I first heard about from Tony Robbins):

1. **Certainty**: The need for security and stability.
2. **Uncertainty/Variety**: The need for excitement and change.

3. **Significance**: The need to feel important and valued.
4. **Love and Connection**: The need to feel close to others.
5. **Growth**: The need to evolve and improve.
6. **Contribution**: The need to give beyond oneself.

Every action—no matter how harmful or misguided—is an attempt to meet one or more of these needs. Even situations like cheating, lying, or selfish behavior—while hurtful—often come from someone's attempt to meet an emotional need. Let's break down a few examples:

- **Cheating**: A way to feel significant or desirable.
- **Lying**: An attempt to gain certainty by avoiding conflict or consequences.
- **Stealing**: A desperate move for certainty—security in the form of money or resources.
- **Addiction**: A way to numb pain and seek connection, even if it's a toxic one with a substance.
- **Violence**: An attempt to regain power and control when someone feels powerless.

Understanding these emotional needs doesn't excuse the behavior. It simply helps us recognize that **people are often acting out of their own unmet needs and pain.**

Remember in Chapter 7 (Key #1), we talked about how everyone is the star of their own movie and how everything we do as human beings is to either gain or avoid a feeling? Well, that's where the "positive intent" part comes into play. It's positive from the perspective that the person doing the harm is trying to solve something within themselves, and everyone else is just a means to an end.

To truly grasp this concept, you have to be willing to accept that you are an extra in other people's movies. Our egos don't like that idea for sure because it wants to be the center of everyone's attention. But that is simply naive.

I said to a client, "If I punched you in the face and robbed you, there was a positive intent in that action. Just not for you. I needed something, and you had it. I'm not thinking about how it would make you feel; I'm thinking about how it would make me feel or serve my needs."

That's hard to accept, isn't it? It feels almost unfair. But consider this, when we hold onto the belief that someone hurt us on purpose, that their actions were solely about causing us pain, we create a narrative that keeps us stuck in resentment, anger, and bitterness. And those emotions, as justified as they feel, are heavy. They keep us chained to the very person or situation we most want to escape.

This isn't about letting go of accountability—it's about letting go of the story that their actions were entirely about you. Because they weren't. What if seeing things this way doesn't just lighten your emotional load but completely changes how you relate to the world around you?

Meet Justin

Justin was the kind of man who turned heads, both on and off the field. As a former professional athlete, he had it all. The accolades, the fame, the lifestyle others could only dream of. But behind the highlight reels and endorsement deals was a man who felt hollow, disconnected, and, frankly, lost.

When Justin retired, it was like someone had turned off the lights. His identity, which had been built entirely around his athletic career, was gone. Without the structure of daily training or the validation of screaming fans, he spiraled. The confidence he once exuded on the field was now replaced with self-doubt and an incessant, critical inner voice.

Justin came to me, reluctantly at first, not because he wanted to change but because his life was falling apart. He drank too much. His relationships were superficial at best and toxic at worst. He admitted he didn't even know how to be a father to his own kids. "What do I have to offer them?" he asked me one day, his voice breaking. "I don't even know who I am anymore."

But as we dug deeper into his story, I discovered there was something even more painful lurking beneath the surface. Justin had been holding onto something that had haunted him for decades—a wound so deep that even his toughest tackles on the field couldn't mask it.

The Secret He Couldn't Forget

Justin revealed that, as a child, he'd been molested by a family friend—someone he trusted, someone who was supposed to protect him. The abuse went on for nearly a year, and when he finally found the courage to tell his parents, his father dismissed it.

"Don't make things up, Justin," his father had said sharply. "We don't need that kind of drama in this family."

Hearing those words from the man who was supposed to protect him shattered Justin. "It was like he chose them over me," Justin said, his fists clenched, his jaw tight. "After that, I learned not to trust anyone. I learned to rely on myself because no one else would."

His father's dismissal became the lens through which Justin viewed the world. It taught him that vulnerability was weakness, that emotions were a liability, and that love was conditional. Justin channeled all of his anger, shame, and grief into sports, where his physical prowess became his armor. On the field, he was invincible. Off the field, he was a man running from his pain.

As Justin sat quietly, I asked him to consider something deeper. "Imagine, for a moment, what it would mean for your father to fully process what you told him. Imagine what it would've felt like for him to face the fact that someone he trusted hurt his child. What do you think that would've done to him emotionally?"

Justin shrugged, his jaw still tight, "He would've had to deal with it. He should have dealt with it."

"You're absolutely right," I said. "But let's step into his shoes for a second. Your father grew up in a world where men weren't taught how to process their emotions. Vulnerability wasn't just frowned upon—it was a threat. For him to believe what you told him, he would've had to face a tidal wave of emotions he was never equipped to handle. Guilt, shame, fear. And maybe, just maybe, the belief that he'd failed as a father."

Justin's eyes narrowed. "But he did fail."

"From your perspective, yes," I said. "But think about what that failure would've meant to him. If he accepted that you were telling the truth, he would've had to face the idea that he wasn't strong enough to protect his own child. That the world wasn't as safe or controllable as he wanted to believe. And that someone he allowed into your life betrayed his trust in the worst possible way. Can you imagine how heavy that would've been for him to carry?"

Justin shifted uncomfortably in his chair but didn't respond.

"Here's the thing," I continued. "Sometimes, people can't face the weight of their own perceived failures, so they deny reality altogether. It's not because they don't care—it's because caring would mean drowning in guilt. By dismissing what you told him, your father wasn't rejecting you. He was trying to protect himself from feelings he didn't know how to process."

I let that sink in before adding, "It's not right. It's not fair. And it's not what you deserved. But it's human."

Justin leaned forward, his forehead resting in his hands. I could see the gears turning in his mind, the defenses he'd built around his pain beginning to crack.

"Think about it, Justin," I said gently. "Your father came from a generation where men were expected to be providers and protectors—strong, stoic, and always in control. Admitting that he failed to protect you would've meant admitting he wasn't the man he thought he was. And that's terrifying. Maybe it was easier for him to convince himself that you were lying than to face the fear that he'd let you down in such a profound way."

Justin's voice was barely above a whisper. "So, he lied to himself?"

"Exactly," I said. "And again, that doesn't make it okay. But it does help us understand why he might have reacted the way he did. He wasn't rejecting you—he was rejecting the story that he'd failed you. Because to him, failure wasn't an option. It was unbearable."

"Imagine what happens to a man like your father when he's confronted with something so painful that he can't face it," I continued. "That denial doesn't just go away. It festers. It eats at him, even if he doesn't show it.

Maybe that's why he was so hard on you later on. Maybe his anger wasn't really about you—it was about the shame he couldn't admit to himself."

Justin looked up, his eyes searching mine. "You think he felt guilty?"

"I don't just think it—I'm sure of it," I said. "But guilt is a heavy thing, Justin. And not everyone knows how to carry it. Some people channel it into anger, others into control. Your father may have been so overwhelmed by his own guilt and shame that he projected it outward instead of dealing with it internally."

Justin sat back, exhaling deeply. "I never thought about it like that. I just thought he didn't care."

I leaned in. "What if he cared so much that it broke him? What if his denial was less about ignoring your pain and more about avoiding his own?"

Why This Matters for Justin's Healing

This shift in perspective wasn't about absolving Justin's father or excusing his reaction. It was about helping Justin understand that his father's response wasn't a reflection of Justin's worth—it was a reflection of his father's limitations.

For Justin, this reframing was a turning point. It didn't erase the hurt or the betrayal, but it softened the edges of his anger. It allowed him to see his father not as a villain, but as a flawed human being—one who made terrible choices, yes, but not because Justin didn't matter.

"Your father's denial wasn't about you," I said. "It was about him. And the more you hold onto the belief that his reaction defined your value, the more power you give him over your life. You can let that go, Justin. Not for his sake, but for yours."

Justin nodded slowly, the weight of decades of pain beginning to lift. For the first time, he could see his father not as the monster he'd built up in his mind, but as a man who struggled with his own demons—demons that had nothing to do with Justin's worth or innocence.

For Justin, this shift was the beginning of his healing. It wasn't about justifying what had happened—it was about understanding that his father's actions (or inactions) were motivated by his own emotional limitations, not by a lack of love for Justin. It allowed him to stop carrying the burden of trying to prove he was enough, because he finally saw that he had always been enough.

Justin's story is a powerful example of how understanding positive intent—no matter how deeply buried or misguided it may be—can help us release the resentment and anger that keep us stuck. It's not about excusing harm. It's about recognizing that other people's actions are a reflection of their own struggles, not a measure of your value. And that's where freedom begins.

A Gentle Note for Those Who Have Experienced Sexual Trauma

I understand that this concept may feel particularly difficult for those who have experienced sexual trauma. **Acknowledging positive intent doesn't mean excusing or minimizing the harm that was done to you.** It's not about saying **what happened** was positive—but **the intent (motive) behind the action** was positive, in some way, for the person committing the action. I know that's not easy to hear, and trust me, I too have had to swallow that pill to gain the peace I have today. Not accepting this only keeps you in emotional turmoil, anger, resentment, and more which only harms you–physically, mentally and emotionally.

The purpose of this chapter is not to diminish your pain but to offer a perspective that might help you release some of the weight you've been carrying. **This is a hard pill to swallow, and I'm not asking you to accept it all at once.** It's okay to take your time with this. Healing isn't about rushing through the pain—it's about shifting your perspective so that it no longer controls you.

Navigating Positive Intent in Everyday Relationships

Okay look, I know that may have been heavy to read. It was heavy to write. But I needed to give space for those who have experienced that level of trauma to be seen, heard and given the opportunity to heal. I also acknowledge that not every hurt comes from those types of traumatic events or deep emotional wounds. Sometimes, the most painful experiences are the subtle betrayals—those moments where someone let us down, didn't show up, or acted selfishly. These kinds of events may not carry the same weight as other situations, but they still leave a lasting mark.

Take, for example, a friend who suddenly distanced themselves without any warning or explanation. From your perspective, it may feel like a betrayal—one day they were there, and the next, they weren't. But from their perspective, their decision might not have been about you at all. Maybe they were overwhelmed with their own life, struggling with personal issues, or afraid of vulnerability. The **positive intent** behind their withdrawal could have been to protect themselves or manage their emotional capacity, not just to hurt you.

Or consider a parent who promised to be at every school recital but only showed up half the time. You might have grown up believing, *"I must not be important enough,"* or, *"If they loved me, they would've been there."* But looking at it from an adult perspective, it's possible that their intent had nothing to do with you. Maybe they were overwhelmed with work, struggling with depression, or dealing with their own unmet emotional needs—trying to survive in ways that weren't visible to you as a child. Their absence wasn't about your worth; it was about what they needed to do in that moment to manage their own life.

When we're hurt by others, it's easy to tell a story that paints them as villains and ourselves as victims. That's not to say the pain isn't real—of course it is. But the key is recognizing that people are often acting based on their own needs, fears, and insecurities—not with the intent to harm you.

This doesn't mean you excuse harmful behavior or let people off the hook. It means you shift your perspective from *"They hurt me on purpose"* to, *"They were doing the best they could for themselves, even though it hurt me."* It's not about condoning the behavior; it's about understanding where it came from so you can begin to release the resentment you've been carrying.

For example, a man I worked with in one of my programs, Marcus, had been to prison three times for breaking into homes. When I asked him why he did it, his answer was simple, *"I needed the money."*

"Why didn't you just get a job?" I asked.

He sighed. "I had a meth problem. I couldn't hold down a job."

I kept pushing. "Why meth? What were you trying to escape?"

This is where Marcus got quiet. After a long pause, he told me that, years ago, a family member had been killed because of something Marcus did. It was gang-related. Marcus had carried the guilt with him ever since, and the only way he knew how to cope was by getting high. "When I'm high," he said, "I don't think about it. I don't feel it."

But getting high came with consequences. When the meth wore off, he felt even worse—not just about his cousin, but about the reckless things he did while high. It was a vicious cycle. He used meth to escape the guilt, but the high made him do things that caused even more guilt. And so, the cycle continued.

Marcus's behavior—breaking into homes, stealing—his actions weren't a positive experience for those getting robbed, but his *intention* wasn't about hurting other people. It was about him trying to meet a need and escape his own pain. That doesn't make his actions right. But it does help us understand them.

Now let's turn this around. It's easy to focus on the ways others have hurt us, but part of this process involves reflecting on how your own actions may have caused pain for others, even when you didn't intend to. Think back to a time when your actions hurt someone else or when you were in survival mode—trying to meet your own needs, even if it meant disappointing someone else. You probably didn't mean to hurt them. Maybe you lied, pushed them away, or acted selfishly. Maybe you canceled plans with a friend because you were overwhelmed, or maybe you weren't fully honest in a relationship because you feared rejection.

What was your intent in those moments? Wasn't it positive for you? Weren't you trying to feel safe, loved, or in control? It's important to recognize that we all have moments where our behavior—motivated by our own needs—ends up hurting someone else.

This reflection isn't about shame or guilt. It's about recognizing the shared human experience. This is where empathy begins—not just for others, but for yourself too. Just like you've hurt others while trying to do what's best for yourself, others have hurt you in the same way. And when you understand that, you begin to see the world—and your pain—through a different lens. You were doing the best you could with the emotional resources you had at the time. And so was everyone else.

A Shift That Sets You Free

Understanding that all human behavior is motivated by positive intent can feel like trying to untangle an impossibly knotted rope. The concept is simple, but applying it requires courage, compassion, and a willingness to look beyond your own story. It's not easy. But let's be real—anything worth having rarely is.

When we talked about Justin earlier, you saw how holding onto anger and resentment toward his father wasn't just hurting his relationships or his identity—it was keeping him locked in a prison of his own making. The same is true for all of us. Resentment, bitterness, and the stories we tell ourselves about why people hurt us act like emotional chains. They bind us to the past and prevent us from living freely in the present.

But here's the gift in understanding positive intent, it's not about letting anyone off the hook—it's about letting yourself off the hook. It's about recognizing that other people's actions are not about you. They're about them—their pain, their unmet needs, their fears, and their limitations. And when you see that, you're no longer carrying the weight of their choices on your shoulders.

To truly embrace this principle, you have to be willing to see beyond your own perspective. It's easy to judge someone else's actions when you're only looking at how those actions affected you. But life isn't that simple. Every person you encounter is navigating their own internal world—a world shaped by their upbringing, experiences, beliefs, and fears. What you see as harm might have been their desperate attempt to feel safe, loved, or valued.

That's the key here: empathy. Not for their actions, but for their humanity. When you see others as human— struggling, and doing the best they can—it becomes easier to let go of the anger and judgment that keep you stuck. And when you do that, you free yourself.

Let's zoom out for a second. Imagine what your life would look like if you truly embraced this principle. Picture yourself letting go of the grudges you've carried for years. Imagine walking through life without the weight of resentment or the sting of betrayal following you like a shadow. That's emotional freedom. That's peace.

Now, take it a step further. When you live from a place of understanding and compassion, it changes how you show up for the people you love. Your kids, your partner, your friends—they'll feel the difference. You'll stop reacting from a place of hurt and start responding from a place of love. And that ripple effect? It doesn't stop with the people closest to you. It spreads outward, touching everyone you encounter.

This is how we change the world—not by pointing fingers, but by choosing to see the humanity in one another. By letting go of the stories that divide us and embracing the truth that we're all just trying to make it through the best way we know how.

At the heart of this chapter—and this book—is the reminder that **you are already whole.** You were born whole. Nothing that's happened to you has changed that. The pain you've endured, the betrayals you've faced, the mistakes you've made—none of it defines your worth. **You are love.** Not because someone else gave it to you, but because it's who you are at your core.

When you fully embody this truth, you stop looking for love and validation outside of yourself. You stop needing others to act a certain way to prove your worth. And in that realization, you become free. Free to forgive. Free to love without fear. Free to live without carrying the burdens of resentment and anger.

The understanding of positive intent isn't just a concept—it's a path to peace. It's a way to reclaim your power and step into the fullness of who you are. So, take this principle, not just as an idea, but as a practice. Apply it in your relationships, your reflections, and your daily life. Let it guide you back to your true self, where you'll find not just peace, but a love so deep and unshakable that it transforms everything it touches.

Because when you truly see yourself as already whole, you'll stop needing others to fill the gaps. And when you stop needing, you'll start giving—not because you have to, but because **you are love**. And love, by its very nature, overflows.

The invitation here isn't to change the people who've hurt you. It's not to erase the past or pretend the pain didn't happen. The invitation is to shift your perspective, to release the chains of resentment, and to choose freedom over bitterness. It's about letting go—not for their sake, but for yours.

The shift is yours to make. And when you do, you'll find that the peace you've been searching for was never out there. It's been within you all along.

Reflective Questions

Take a moment to reflect:

- When have your actions hurt someone, even though you didn't intend to?
- What emotional need were you trying to meet in those moments?
- What behavior have you taken personally from others? What needs might have been driving their actions?
- What are you still holding onto? What story are you ready to release today?
- What might your life look like if you allowed yourself to see the world, not through the lens of hurt, but through the lens of love?

Chapter 13

Key #7: We Judge Others by Their Actions, Ourselves by Our Intentions

Let's talk about something we all do, but rarely admit—even to ourselves. You know that moment when someone cuts you off in traffic? Your blood boils, and without hesitation, you've got them all figured out, *"What a reckless idiot! How does someone like that even get a license?"* You've built their whole personality in a matter of seconds: careless, selfish, probably a terrible person overall.

But let's flip the script. When *you're* the one who accidentally cuts someone off? Oh, well, *that's* different. *"I didn't see them! I wasn't trying to be rude—I just misjudged the lane change. Everyone makes mistakes!"* See the difference? In one scenario, their actions define their entire character. In the other, your intentions save you from judgment.

We all live inside our own heads, so of course, it feels natural to judge ourselves based on what we *meant* to do. After all, you know your own heart. You know you weren't trying to hurt anyone or be disrespectful—you just had a moment. But when it comes to everyone else? All you see are their actions. You don't know their backstory, their intentions, or the pressures they're carrying. So, instead of offering grace, you fill in the blanks with assumptions—and let's be real, those assumptions aren't usually generous.

Think about it. If a friend owes you money and hasn't paid it back, your mind jumps to, *"Wow, they're so inconsiderate. This is exactly why I don't lend money."* But when *you* owe someone money? *"I've just been so tight lately. I'll pay them back as soon as I can—they'll understand."*

Or take relationships. If someone breaks your trust, the story you tell yourself is something like, *"They're heartless and selfish!"* But if you're the one who betrays someone's trust? *"I didn't mean for this to happen. Things just got so complicated, and I was feeling lost."*

Sound familiar? It's okay—this about helping you see something most of us are completely blind to: we judge others based solely on what they *do*, but we judge ourselves based on what we *meant* to do. And that double standard? It's not just unfair—it's the root of so many conflicts in our lives.

We carry this mindset into every relationship we have. Our marriages, our friendships, even our relationships with our parents and kids. We get frustrated with other people for their actions, but we demand that they understand our intentions. And when they don't? It feels like betrayal.

If you're carrying frustration, resentment, or hurt because of what someone else did, there's a good chance they're carrying the same feelings toward you. Not because they're evil or out to get you, but because they're doing the same thing you are—they're judging you by your actions while expecting you to understand their intentions.

This double standard isn't just some random quirk of human nature—it's everywhere. It's in our friendships, our marriages, and most definitely in our parenting. And it's sneaky, too. You don't even realize you're doing it until someone holds up a mirror. That's exactly what happened with Simone.

Meet Simone

Simone is the kind of woman who seems to have it all figured out. At 42, she's one of the top attorneys at a prestigious law firm. Her days are a blur of back-to-back meetings, courtroom battles, and late-night strategy sessions. People admire her drive, her discipline, and her flawless ability to command a room.

But when Simone came to me, she wasn't here to talk about her career. She was here because of Caleb, her 10-year-old son.

"I don't know what to do with him anymore," she said, the frustration clear in her voice. "He doesn't listen, he doesn't care about school, and he's constantly glued to that stupid video game. It's like he's given up on life before it's even started."

She paused, her tone softening. "I just don't understand him. I'm working so hard to give him a better life, and he acts like it doesn't matter."

Simone described their most recent argument.

"I asked him to clean his room three times," she said. "When he didn't, I called him lazy, and he yelled back that I care more about my job than I do about him. He slammed the door, and I just stood there. I couldn't believe he had the nerve to say that after everything I've sacrificed for him."

She leaned forward, her frustration now giving way to guilt. "I don't want to be this kind of mom. I don't want Caleb to feel like I don't care. But I don't know how to get through to him."

Simone's life is tightly wound around her career. Her job isn't just a job—it's her identity. She tells herself that her long hours and relentless pursuit of success are all for Caleb, to give him the kind of life she never had. But deep down, she knows that's not the whole story. Work is where she feels in control, where she feels seen, where she feels like she's enough.

At home, it's a different story. Caleb barely talks to her, their conversations usually ending in arguments. She sees him as unmotivated and aimless, qualities that terrify her. "What kind of future is he going to have if he doesn't care about anything?" she asked me during one session.

Caleb isn't lazy—he's overwhelmed. His mother's constant pressure feels suffocating, and in his own way, he's pulling back, retreating into a world where he doesn't have to measure up.

The truth is, Caleb doesn't see Simone's sacrifices—he sees her absence. He doesn't understand her intentions, only her actions. And when Simone snaps at him, he doesn't hear, "I want you to succeed." He hears, "You're not enough."

Simone's relationship with Caleb is a reflection of the one she had with her father, though she doesn't realize it yet.

Her father was a hardworking man who juggled multiple jobs to make ends meet. He was a delivery driver by day and a janitor by night, often coming home too tired to engage with Simone or her siblings.

"He was always working," she told me. "And when he was home, he didn't have time for us. I'd try to show him my report card or talk to him about my day, and he'd just say, 'Not now, Simone. I'm busy.'"

As a child, Simone interpreted this as indifference. She convinced herself that she had to earn her father's love through achievements—Straight A's, trophies, scholarships—but none of it seemed to break through his wall of exhaustion and stress.

"I thought if I worked hard enough, he'd finally notice me," she said. "But no matter what I did, it was never enough."

That belief—that love is something you earn—became the foundation of Simone's identity. It drove her to succeed but also left her chasing a sense of worth she could never quite catch.

Now, she's unintentionally passing that same pressure onto Caleb. She thinks she's teaching him responsibility, but Caleb feels the same invisible weight Simone once carried: the fear of never being enough.

When Simone walked into my office, she was convinced that Caleb was the problem. "He needs to learn discipline," she said. "He needs to understand that life isn't handed to you on a silver platter."

But as we dug deeper, it became clear that Simone wasn't just fighting with Caleb—she was fighting with her past. Her father's absence still haunted her, shaping how she saw herself and, in turn, how she saw Caleb.

"Do you think Caleb might feel about you the way you felt about your father?" I asked during one session.

Her eyes widened, the question catching her off guard. "I don't know," she said quietly. "I've never thought about it like that."

We Judge Actions, Excuse Intentions

Simone's story is the perfect example.

Convinced Caleb was the problem, she thought she had him all figured out: he was lazy, unmotivated, and completely apathetic about life. She saw his actions—avoiding chores, playing video games, and showing zero interest in school—and built his entire personality around them.

The twist was that Simone was doing the exact same thing Caleb was.

Caleb avoided chores to escape what felt like impossible expectations. Simone buried herself in work to avoid the vulnerability of showing up emotionally. Caleb checked out because he felt like nothing he did was good enough. Simone poured everything into her career because she still believed she had to earn her worth.

The only difference? Caleb's behavior was visible, while Simone's was masked as "sacrifice."

When I pointed this out to her, Simone was quick to defend herself. "But I'm doing it for him! I'm working hard to give him opportunities."

"And Caleb's playing video games because it's the only place where he feels like he's succeeding," I said. "Do you see how, in his world, that makes sense?"

She sat back, stunned. For the first time, she realized she'd been holding Caleb to a standard she wasn't living up to herself. She'd judged his actions but excused her own intentions.

Let's be honest—Simone isn't the only one who does this. We all do it.

Think about the last time someone hurt or frustrated you. Maybe they ignored your texts, showed up late, or forgot something important. How quickly did you jump to conclusions about their character? *"They don't care," "They don't value me,"* or *"They're selfish."*

Now flip the script. When you've done the same thing—forgotten a birthday, been late to a meeting, let someone down—what story did you tell yourself? *"I've been so busy," "I didn't mean to,"* or *"They'll understand."*

See how easy it is to let yourself off the hook while holding others to a higher standard? That's the double standard we're talking about. It's not just unfair—it's a relationship killer.

When we judge others by their actions but excuse ourselves with our intentions, we create a wall of frustration and resentment. It's a wall that keeps us from seeing the other person's humanity—their struggles, their fears, their reasons.

For Simone, this wall had been growing between her and Caleb for years. She saw his actions as a reflection of his character, not as a response to the pressure he felt. Caleb, in turn, saw her absence, not her intentions. They were stuck in a cycle of misjudgment, each feeling unseen and misunderstood.

Let's pause for a moment. Think about someone you're frustrated with right now. Maybe it's your partner, your kid, a coworker, or even a friend. Ask yourself, what actions are you judging them for? What story have you created about their character based on those actions? Now, flip the lens, if you were in their shoes, what might their intentions be? What pressures, fears, or needs might be driving their behavior?

This isn't about excusing harmful behavior—it's about recognizing that people are more than their actions. Just like you are.

This shift in perspective isn't easy, but recognizing the hypocrisy in judging others is a game-changer. When Simone started to see Caleb not as lazy but as overwhelmed, their relationship began to shift. But there's more to the story—because understanding someone's intentions requires something even harder than self-awareness. It requires stepping out of your own narrative and seeking to understand theirs.

Most conflicts don't start with malice—they start with misunderstanding. We're so wrapped up in defending our intentions and proving our point that we forget to pause and ask, "What's really going on with them?"

Simone was stuck in this exact cycle with Caleb. She was so focused on her sacrifices—how much she was doing for him—that she never stopped to think about how her actions felt from his perspective. To her, being a hardworking mom was a badge of honor. But to Caleb, it felt like he came second to her job.

"He doesn't appreciate anything I do for him," she said during one session.

"What do you think he sees when you're working late, missing his soccer games, or glued to your laptop at dinner?" I asked.

Simone hesitated. "I don't know... maybe that I don't care?"

"Exactly," I said. "Caleb isn't seeing your sacrifices—he's seeing your absence. He's interpreting your actions, not your intentions."

For the first time, Simone realized she'd been so busy trying to be understood—convincing Caleb that her hard work was for him—that she'd never tried to understand what her actions felt like to him.

We all do this. When we feel unappreciated, misunderstood, or hurt, our first instinct is to defend ourselves, *"You don't get it! Here's why I'm right!"* But that approach rarely works. Why? Because the other person is doing the exact same thing—defending themselves and waiting for you to understand *them.*

It's like two people shouting through megaphones at the same time. No one's listening, and no one's being heard.

To break the cycle, someone has to go first. Someone has to put down their megaphone and say, "Help me understand your perspective." That doesn't mean you're wrong or that your feelings don't matter. It just means you're willing to lead with curiosity instead of judgment.

Think of a conflict like a game of tug-of-war. Both sides are pulling as hard as they can, trying to win. But the second one person lets go of the rope, the whole dynamic changes. Instead of a battle, it becomes a conversation. That's what happens when you choose to understand first—you let go of the rope.

The next time you find yourself in a conflict, try this:

1. **Pause:** Before reacting, take a breath and remind yourself: *Their actions aren't the whole story.*
2. **Ask:** Instead of defending your position, ask a question like:
   - "Can you help me understand why you feel this way?"
   - "What's going on for you that made you act this way?"
3. **Listen:** Really listen—not to respond, but to understand.
4. **Reflect:** Once they've shared their perspective, repeat back what you heard: "So what you're saying is…"

Simone started practicing this with Caleb. Instead of jumping straight into frustration when he ignored her requests, she asked him what was going on. At first, Caleb was defensive, but eventually, he opened up.

"I feel like nothing I do is ever enough for you," he admitted one night after an argument.

That hit Simone like a ton of bricks. Caleb wasn't lazy—he was overwhelmed. He felt like he could never meet her expectations, so he'd stopped trying altogether.

By seeking to understand Caleb's perspective, Simone didn't just change the way she saw him—she changed the way Caleb saw her. Their conversations shifted from battles to bridges, creating a foundation for the deeper work they both needed to do.

Understanding someone's perspective is powerful, but it's not the whole story. We think we're speaking the same language as the people around us, but often, we're not. The same words, actions, or gestures can mean entirely different things to different people. And those differences? That's where so much of our conflict begins. Miscommunication.

We all assign meaning to words and actions based on our own experiences, values, and emotions. Just because *you* mean something one way doesn't mean the person you're talking to interprets it the same way.

Take Simone, for example. She thought she was teaching Caleb responsibility by calling him "lazy" when he didn't clean his room. To her, it was a push to do better, a wake-up call. But to Caleb, the word "lazy" didn't mean "you can improve." It meant "you're not good enough."

When Simone and I unpacked this in one of our sessions, she was stunned. "I never thought about how he might hear that word," she admitted. "To me, it's just about not trying hard enough."

"Exactly," I said. "But to Caleb, it's an attack on who he is, not what he does. That one word carries years of expectations and frustration—and none of it feels good."

This is the danger of assumptions. We think our words are clear, but clarity is subjective. Without checking in, we create gaps between what we mean and what others hear.

The Power Is In The Listener

Think about the last time someone misunderstood you. Maybe you said something you thought was harmless, but it sparked an argument. Or maybe someone did something you found hurtful, but they were confused about why you were upset.

Chances are, the problem wasn't what was said or done—it was the meaning each of you assigned to it.

Here's how it happens:

1. **You speak or act based on your intentions.**
    - Example: You say, "I need some space," meaning you're overwhelmed and need time to think.
2. **They interpret it through their lens.**
    - They hear, "I'm mad at you" or "I'm pulling away," based on their past experiences or fears.

Neither of you is wrong—but neither of you is right, either. The truth is, *the power is in the listener.* As my good friend Steve Hardison says, "It's not what's said—it's what's heard that creates reality."

The listener's interpretation—their lens—is what gives words meaning. And their lens is shaped by their upbringing, past experiences, and emotional state. That's why the same word can hit two people in completely different ways.

The problem isn't just what was said—it's how it was heard. And the only way to close that gap is to stop assuming you're on the same page and start clarifying.

Miscommunication is like two people using different GPS apps to get to the same destination. One app says, 'Turn left,' the other says, 'Go straight,' and before you know it, you're lost and blaming each other for being off track. The problem isn't the route—it's that you didn't sync your directions before you started.

Here's how to start closing the gap between what you mean and what others hear:

1. **Ask for Clarity:**
   - Instead of assuming you both are on the same page, ask questions like:
     - "When you say X, what do you mean?"
     - "How does that word feel to you?"
   - Example: Simone could ask Caleb, "What do you think I mean when I say 'lazy'?"
2. **Explain Your Meaning:**
   - Don't assume they know what you mean. Spell it out:
     - "When I say X, I'm trying to say…"
   - Example: Simone could say, "When I call you lazy, I'm not saying you're a bad person. I'm saying I believe you're capable of so much more."
3. **Repeat What You Heard:**
   - After they explain their meaning, repeat it back to make sure you're on the same page:
     - "So, what you're saying is…"

Simone started practicing this with Caleb. One evening, instead of accusing him of being lazy, she asked, "When I say that word, how does it make you feel?"

Caleb hesitated before answering. "Like I'll never be good enough for you," he said quietly.

Simone felt like she'd been hit by a truck. She'd been using the word to push Caleb forward, but instead, it had been pulling him down.

From that point on, she started clarifying her words and asking Caleb to do the same. Slowly, they began to bridge the gap that had been growing between them.

Ditch Expectations, Build Agreements

Now miscommunication is one thing, but expectations take it to a whole new level. We place them on everyone—our kids, our partners, our friends, our coworkers—and then we get upset when they don't meet them. Most of the time, they didn't even know the expectations existed.

If you think about it, you don't want anyone to have expectations of you either. Expectations are a one-sided setup for disappointment. Agreements, on the other hand? Agreements are where real connection happens.

The truth is, expecting someone to meet your unspoken standards is unfair—to them and to you. It's like giving someone a test they didn't know they were taking and then being furious when they fail.

Let's look at Simone, for example.

Simone expected Caleb to value hard work and discipline the same way she did. She thought he should know that keeping his room clean and excelling in school were non-negotiables. After all, isn't that just common sense?

But Caleb didn't know these were expectations. To him, "clean your room" wasn't about responsibility—it was another way he felt like he couldn't measure up.

When I asked Simone, "Do you want Caleb to have expectations of you that he never communicates?" she shook her head.

"Of course not," she said.

"Then why is it okay for you to have them of him?" I asked.

That question hit her hard. For the first time, Simone realized that she wasn't just setting herself up for disappointment—she was setting Caleb up for failure.

Here's the problem with expectations, first off, they're one-sided. Expectations come from *your* perspective, with no input from the other person. Second, they're unspoken. Most of the time, we don't even communicate them. Third, they set the stage for failure. When people don't meet our expectations, we feel let down—even if they never agreed to them in the first place.

Steve Chandler puts it perfectly: expectations are assumptions; agreements are collaborations.

Expectations say:

- "You should know what I want without me telling you."
- "You're wrong if you don't meet my standards."

Agreements say:

- "Let's talk about what we both need and how we can work together to create it."
- "Here's what I'd like. Does that work for you?"

Expectations are rooted in control. Agreements are rooted in connection. And when you stop expecting and start agreeing, everything changes.

Having expectations is like giving someone a set of rules they've never seen and then getting mad when they break them. Building agreements, on the other hand, is like sitting down together to write the rules in a way that works for both of you.

Here's how to move from expectations to agreements:

1. **Recognize Your Expectations:**
    - Ask yourself, "What am I expecting from this person that I haven't clearly communicated or collaborated on?"
2. **Initiate the Conversation:**
    - Instead of assuming they know, bring it up:

- "I'd like to talk about what we both need in this situation. Can we make an agreement about how to move forward?"

3. **Collaborate, Don't Dictate:**
    - Let go of control and focus on finding something that works for both of you.
        - Instead of expecting Caleb to clean his room "because I said so," Simone could say, "Keeping the house clean is important to me. What's a way we can work together on this that feels fair to you?"

4. **Commit to the Agreement:**
    - Agreements are only powerful if both sides take ownership. Once you've agreed, honor it—and hold the other person accountable for doing the same.

When Simone shifted from expectations to agreements, her relationship with Caleb started to transform.

Instead of saying, "You need to do better in school," she said, "What can we agree on when it comes to your homework? What do you need from me to help you succeed?"

At first, Caleb was hesitant. He wasn't used to being asked for his input. But over time, he began to open up. "I just want you to notice when I try," he said.

That simple conversation led to a breakthrough. Instead of demanding perfection, Simone agreed to focus on encouraging Caleb's efforts. And Caleb agreed to work on his chores and homework without her nagging.

Emotions Are Valid, But They're Not Facts

Here's the thing about "I feel" statements, they're often disguised accusations.

- "I feel like you don't care about me."
- "I feel like you're lazy."
- "I feel like you're never listening."

Sound familiar?

The problem with these statements is that they're not actually about feelings—they're judgments wrapped in emotional language. And when you throw them at someone, their natural response is to get defensive. Because what you're really saying is, "You're the problem."

But here's the truth, feelings aren't facts. They're the result of your thoughts. And if you want to have a productive conversation, you have to get to the thought behind the feeling.

How "I Feel" Creates an Emotional Spiral

In one session, Simone said, "I feel like Caleb doesn't respect me. He doesn't listen, he doesn't do what I ask, and it's like nothing I do matters to him."

"Okay," I said, "but is that a feeling, or is it a thought?"

Simone paused, confused. "What do you mean?"

"Let's break it down. You feel disrespected, but what's the thought behind that feeling? What's Caleb doing that makes you think he doesn't respect you?"

"Well, he ignores me when I ask him to do things, and he talks back," she said.

"Got it," I said. "Let's seek to understand before wanting to be understood. Have you ever tuned someone out or didn't listen?"

"Yes," she replied.

"And what was the reason?" I asked her.

"Because I was frustrated and overwhelmed," she said.

"Now let's reframe that. Instead of saying, 'I feel like Caleb doesn't respect me,' what if you said, 'I think Caleb doesn't listen because he's frustrated or overwhelmed'? See how that can shift the conversation? But remember, we are making a guess on what he might be feeling, you still have to get clarity from him and actually ask," I said.

By reframing her statement, Simone moved from an emotional accusation to a thoughtful observation. And when she approached Caleb with this new mindset, their conversation went differently. Instead of shutting down, Caleb opened up.

Here's why this shift is so powerful:

1. **It Creates Clarity:**
   - Feelings can be vague or misleading, but thoughts can be explored and discussed.
2. **It Reduces Defensiveness:**
   - "I feel like you don't care" puts someone on trial.
   - "I think you're overwhelmed" invites understanding.
3. **It Promotes Problem-Solving:**
   - Emotional spirals keep you stuck. Reframing leads to productive conversations.

Feelings are like smoke—they tell you there's a fire, but they don't tell you where it's coming from. To put out the fire, you have to look past the smoke and find the source. Reframing 'I feel' statements is how you get to the root of the problem. Here's how you do that:

1. **Identify the Feeling:**
   - Start with the raw emotion: Are you sad, frustrated, hurt, or angry?
2. **Find the Thought Behind It:**
   - Ask yourself, "What am I thinking that's creating this feeling?"
   - Example: "I feel unappreciated because I think they don't notice my efforts."
3. **Reframe the Statement:**
   - Shift from "I feel" to "I think," "I believe," or "I know."
   - Example: Instead of "I feel like you don't care," say, "I think you're distracted, and it's making me feel ignored."
4. **Invite Collaboration:**

- After reframing, ask: "Does that sound accurate to you? Can we talk about it?"

After learning how to reframe her "I feel" statements, Simone tried it with Caleb.

Instead of saying, "I feel like you don't respect me," she said, "I think you're overwhelmed when I ask you to do chores. Can we talk about what's making you feel that way?"

Caleb was caught off guard. Instead of lashing out, he admitted he felt like he was drowning under the workload and didn't feel like he had the space to just be a kid.

That one shift—from accusation to collaboration—changed the tone of their entire conversation. For the first time, Simone and Caleb started to understand each other.

The Cost of "Should" Thinking

You've learned how to reframe "I feel" statements to create clarity and connection. But what happens when the root of your frustration isn't just miscommunication or unmet needs? What if it's the constant battle between reality and your expectations of how things "should" be? Spoiler alert: "should" is the sneakiest troublemaker of them all.

If you've ever found yourself thinking, *"They should know better"*, or *"This shouldn't be happening"*, or *"Life shouldn't be this hard"*, you've fallen into the "should" trap. And you're not alone.

"Should" is seductive. It feels righteous, even justified. But the problem is that every time you argue with reality, reality wins. The gap between what *is* and what you think *should* be is where frustration, resentment, and suffering thrive.

Let me break it down:

- **Reality:** Caleb plays video games after school and doesn't prioritize his homework.

- **Simone's "Should":** "He should want to succeed in school like I did."

The gap between those two things wasn't motivating Caleb—it was driving Simone mad. She spent so much time focused on how Caleb *should* act that she wasn't dealing with how he *was* acting. And that mindset kept her stuck in frustration.

I'll give you three reasons why "should" is so dangerous. Number one, it keeps you stuck in judgment. When you focus on how things "should" be, you miss the opportunity to address how they actually are. Number two, it blocks empathy. Thinking, *"They should know better"* shuts down curiosity. Thinking, *"What's going on with them?"* opens the door to understanding. Number three, it creates emotional resistance. Fighting reality doesn't change reality—it just drains your energy.

In one session, Simone vented, "Caleb should care about his future. He should want to do well in school. He should listen to me when I tell him what's best for him."

I let her finish and then asked, "What if Caleb's reality doesn't match your 'should'? What if he's doing the best he can with where he is right now?"

Simone stared at me, silent for a moment. "But if I don't hold him to a higher standard, he'll never succeed," she said.

"Simone," I said gently, "there's a difference between guiding Caleb and rejecting his reality. You can help him grow without expecting him to live by your rulebook. What if, instead of focusing on what he *should* be, you focused on who he *is*?"

That question shifted something in Simone. She realized that her "shoulds" weren't motivating Caleb—they were making him feel judged and disconnected. By letting go of her "shoulds," she could meet Caleb where he was and help him move forward without resentment.

The key is, letting go of "should" doesn't mean giving up on change. It means accepting reality as the starting point for growth.

When you stop arguing with how things are, you free yourself to actually do something about it.

For example, instead of, "They *should* understand my needs," try, "Right now, they don't understand my needs. How can I express them more clearly?" Or, instead of, "This *shouldn't* be happening," try, "This is happening. What's the next best step I can take?"

Acceptance isn't resignation—it's clarity. It's about seeing reality for what it is, not what you wish it were, so you can move forward with purpose.

Fighting reality is like standing in the rain and yelling at the clouds to go away. You're not going to stop the rain—but you can grab an umbrella and keep moving. Accepting reality is the umbrella that lets you navigate life without getting soaked.

Here's practical steps to start letting go of "should":

1. **Catch Your "Shoulds":**
    - Notice when you think or say, "They should…," "This shouldn't…," or "I shouldn't have to…"
2. **Ask Yourself:**
    - "What is the reality of this situation?"
    - "How can I work with what's happening, instead of fighting it?"
3. **Reframe Your Thoughts:**
    - Shift from "should" to acceptance.
        - Example: "They should know better" becomes "They're doing the best they can with what they know right now."
4. **Focus on the Next Step:**
    - Once you accept reality, ask, "What's one thing I can do to improve this situation?"

Simone started practicing this with Caleb. Instead of focusing on how he "should" act, she asked herself, "What's his reality right now?"

When Caleb ignored his homework to play video games, she didn't say, "You should care more about school." Instead, she said, "What's going on for you right now? Are you feeling stuck with your assignments?"

By meeting Caleb where he was, Simone found opportunities to guide him without judgment. And Caleb, feeling seen and understood, became more open to her guidance.

The Generational Shift: A Timeline of Progress

Letting go of "should" helps you accept reality and work with what's in front of you. But what happens when that reality isn't just yours? What if the patterns and beliefs you're battling have been passed down through generations? Here's where we dive into one of the most profound lessons of all: the generational shift. This is about understanding where you come from, consciously deciding where you're going, and giving credit where it's due.

No one starts life with a clean slate. We inherit beliefs, habits, and emotional patterns from our families—some empowering, others limiting. And whether you realize it or not, you're moving the needle forward for the next generation.

I often draw a timeline for clients that looks something like this:

$$-10 \rightarrow -5 \rightarrow 0 \rightarrow +5 \rightarrow +10$$

Think of it like this, if your parents grew up in a "-10" environment—poverty, trauma, neglect—they might have moved the needle to a "-5" for you. It wasn't perfect, but it was progress. Now, your job is to take it further, maybe to "0" or even a "+5", so your kids can have a better starting point than you did.

But here's the thing, most of us don't give our parents credit for the progress they made.

Instead, we judge them for not raising us in a "+5" or "+10" environment. We compare their parenting to what we now know is possible, forgetting that they were working with fewer tools, less information, and often a lot more personal struggle.

Simone's father worked multiple jobs to make ends meet, and he was rarely home. When he was around, he was exhausted, emotionally unavailable, and quick to dismiss Simone's feelings.

"I always felt like I didn't matter," she told me during one session. "No matter how hard I worked in school or how many awards I won, it was like he didn't care."

Simone resented him for years. She saw his absence as proof that she wasn't important to him. But what she didn't see was the progress he had already made compared to his own upbringing.

"Simone," I said, "what do you know about your father's childhood?"

She paused. "Not much," she admitted. "He didn't talk about it much, but I know his dad wasn't around."

"Exactly," I said. "Your father might not have been emotionally present for you, but he showed up in ways his own father never did. To him, putting a roof over your head and food on the table was moving the needle. That was his way of showing love, even if it wasn't in the way you needed. He was doing the best he could with what he had."

For Simone's father, holding down a steady job and keeping his family together was progress. It was his way of breaking the cycle of instability and neglect he grew up with. But Simone could only see his actions, she couldn't see his intentions.

And that's the unfairness of it all. We hold our parents accountable to the standards of a world they were never exposed to.

Let's be clear, this isn't about excusing harm or minimizing your pain. It's about recognizing the reality of progress—and the fact that progress often happens in small, imperfect steps.

Here's why this matters:

1. **Your Parents Did the Best They Could with the Tools They Had:**
    - As mentioned before in Key #4, your parents likely weren't raised with the parenting books, research, and emotional resources that exist today. They parented you based on what they knew—and for many of them, that was better than what they experienced.
2. **Progress Isn't Always Visible:**

- If your parents grew up in chaos, simply creating a stable home might have been a huge leap forward. If they never felt loved as a child, working hard to provide for you might have been their way of showing love—even if it wasn't how you needed it.
3. **You Don't Know Their Full Story:**
    - Without understanding the environment they came from, it's impossible to fully appreciate how far they've come.

For Simone, acknowledging her father's progress was a turning point. She realized that her resentment wasn't just about what he didn't do—it was about her lack of understanding of what he *did* do.

"When I think about it," she said during one session, "my dad never had the chance to go to school. He was working to help his family when he was younger than Caleb is now. Just being there for us, even in his limited way, was something he never had for himself."

That shift didn't erase Simone's pain, but it softened the edges of her anger. It allowed her to see her father not as the villain of her story, but as a man doing his best to break his own cycle.

And that understanding gave her the clarity to approach Caleb differently. Breaking the cycle isn't just about doing the work yourself—it's about bringing your kids into the process.

One of the biggest mistakes parents make is thinking they need to shield their kids from the changes they're making. *"They're too young to understand,"* parents say, or, *"I don't want to burden them."* But the reality is, kids are meaning-making machines. If you don't explain what's happening, they'll create their own meanings—ones that are often inaccurate, self-critical, or downright harmful.

Simone learned this the hard way. Caleb had started asking questions, like, "Why do you work so much?" or "Why can't we hang out more?" Instead of answering him honestly, she brushed it off, thinking, *"He's too young to understand why I'm working so hard."*

But what Caleb heard was, *"Mom doesn't care about spending time with me."*

When I encouraged Simone to start explaining her choices to Caleb, everything changed.

During one dinner, she said, "I want to tell you why I work so hard. When I was a kid, we didn't have much, and my dad worked a lot to make sure we were okay. I've always wanted to give you a life where you don't have to worry about those things. But I also realize that sometimes, I'm not as present as I could be. I'm working on that, and I need your help. Can we figure this out together?"

Caleb's response floored her. "I just want you to play with me more. I don't care about all the other stuff."

That moment of honesty created a bridge. By explaining the cycle, she was breaking and inviting Caleb into the process, Simone gave him the tools to understand their relationship—and his own power to move the needle even further.

This chapter isn't just about breaking cycles—it's about seeing the bigger picture. When you understand the progress your parents made, you stop judging them solely by their actions and start seeing their intent.

Just like Simone judged Caleb for his actions without understanding his struggles, we often judge our parents for what they didn't do without understanding what they overcame. And when we do that, we perpetuate the very cycles we're trying to break.

By choosing to understand rather than judge—whether it's your parents, your kids, or even yourself—you create a space for healing. And in that space, the needle moves forward.

Simone's Life After the Breakthrough

Simone's transformation didn't happen overnight, but the shift was undeniable. By releasing the need to judge Caleb by his actions and starting to understand his intentions, she began to see him not as a problem to fix but as a person to connect with. The tension in their relationship started to melt away—not because Caleb suddenly became the perfect student or cleaned his room without being asked, but because Simone stopped trying to make him fit into her expectations.

She became more intentional about spending time with Caleb, not as a reward for his behavior but as a way to strengthen their bond. The more she invested in simply being present, the more Caleb opened up. His walls of defensiveness began to come down, replaced by a growing trust that his mom saw him for who he truly was, not just who she wanted him to be.

At work, Simone also noticed a change. Her conversations with colleagues became more collaborative, her leadership style more inclusive. She realized that the grace she was learning to extend to Caleb also applied to her team. Instead of micromanaging or assuming the worst, she started asking more questions, listening more deeply, and creating agreements that worked for everyone involved.

The most profound shift, however, was within Simone herself. She stopped seeing her worth as something she had to earn—through her career, her parenting, or her sacrifices. Instead, she realized she was already whole and always had been. That newfound sense of self allowed her to approach life with more compassion, more patience, and—most importantly—more peace.

Simone's breakthrough wasn't just about Caleb. It was about breaking the generational patterns that had shaped her view of love, success, and connection. And as she healed those patterns within herself, she gave Caleb permission to do the same.

A Shift That Sets You Free

So, what does all this mean for you? How do Simone's struggles and breakthroughs translate into your own life? The truth is, we all have our "Calebs"—people we judge by their actions while excusing ourselves with our intentions. Maybe it's your partner who didn't follow through on a promise, a friend who seems distant, or even your own kids who just don't seem to "get it." The double standard of judging others by what they do while expecting them to understand your heart? That's the very thing keeping you stuck.

The shift that sets you free starts with stepping out of this cycle. It's about recognizing that your assumptions about others' actions aren't the full story. Just as your intentions don't always translate perfectly into your actions, neither do theirs. By embracing this, you create a bridge—one built on curiosity, understanding, and connection.

What if you paused before assigning judgment? What if, instead of assuming someone's actions define them, you chose to wonder about their intentions? What if, instead of defending your own intentions, you focused on showing them clearly through your actions? This isn't about letting people off the hook or excusing harmful behavior—it's about seeing the humanity in others, just as you hope they'll see it in you.

The freedom comes in letting go of the story you've created about someone else's actions and choosing to engage with their reality instead. It comes in realizing that understanding someone else doesn't mean agreeing with them—it means respecting their perspective enough to listen.

When you do this, you're not just transforming your relationships—you're transforming yourself. You're moving out of the prison of resentment, frustration, and misunderstanding into a space where connection and peace are possible. Because at the end of the day, the shift isn't just about them—it's about you, and your willingness to see the world through a wider, more compassionate lens. That's the path to emotional freedom, and it starts right here.

Reflective Questions

Take a moment to reflect:

- Think of a recent disagreement or conflict in your life. How might the other person's intentions differ from the story you've created about their actions?
- Are there areas in your life where you're holding others to expectations they don't know about? How can you turn those expectations into agreements?
- What "shoulds" are you holding onto that are keeping you stuck? How can you reframe them to align with reality?

- How do you currently assign meaning to the words or actions of others? Are you clarifying or assuming?
- When was the last time you explained your own intentions clearly? How did that change the outcome of the situation?
- In what ways have generational patterns shaped how you interact with the people closest to you? What steps can you take to consciously break or evolve those patterns?
- How can you create space in your relationships to better understand the intentions behind others' actions?

Chapter 14

Key #8: Respect Other People's Way of Seeing the World (Even If You Don't Understand It)

Have you ever noticed how easy it is to get frustrated with someone because they see things so differently than you do? Whether it's in the workplace, your family, or a simple conversation, when someone doesn't share your perspective, it can feel like a wall goes up between you. You know, like when you're talking to a friend who just doesn't get what you're saying, and you're thinking, how can they be so blind?

We all see the world through our own lens. Every belief, every value we have has been shaped by our experiences, our upbringing, our relationships—our entire lives. And, just like you've walked your own path, so has everyone else. The challenge, though, is to respect that their way of seeing the world is just as valid to them as yours is to you—even when you don't understand it.

But what happens when we don't? What happens when we hold so tightly to our own perspective that we can't—or won't—see anyone else's? It's easy to feel like the problem is everyone else. *"They're too sensitive,"* or, *"They're just being unreasonable."* But that rigidity—the refusal to consider another viewpoint—can cost us more than we realize.

Not respecting others' ways of seeing the world doesn't just create distance between you and them—it creates your own suffering. The more you insist that everyone must think and act the way you do, the more frustrated, isolated, and resentful you become. You trap yourself in a cycle of conflict and tension, shutting out the peace that comes from connection and understanding.

One of my favorite masterclasses was by Condoleezza Rice and Madeleine Albright on diplomacy. These two women sat down with leaders from countries where their very presence was offensive. Imagine having to negotiate with someone who doesn't even think you should be in the room.

They don't respect you, and they certainly don't respect your gender. But to do their jobs, they had to look past that—they had to understand those leaders' worldview, even if they didn't agree with it.

Madeleine Albright put it perfectly when she said, "If I didn't learn to respect other people's ways of seeing the world, I wouldn't have been able to do my job."

This is what diplomacy is all about: understanding—not necessarily agreeing, but understanding. You don't have to change your worldview, but recognizing someone else's is essential for creating common ground.

Now, let's take that lesson and apply it to our everyday lives. When we fail to respect another person's worldview, we're not just hurting them—we're hurting ourselves. We're blocking peace, and that's a surefire way to keep ourselves stuck in unnecessary tension.

But how do we actually practice this respect in the world outside of politics and diplomacy? And why is it so hard?

Let's start with something that's probably a little closer to home, family dynamics. We've all been there. Maybe it's a parent who disapproves of your life choices. Maybe it's an adult child who has chosen a different path from what you had imagined for them. How many times have you looked at your kids or parents and thought, how could they not see what I'm trying to do here? Or why can't they understand where I'm coming from?

It's tough, right? When someone you love and respect doesn't understand or agree with your decisions, it can feel like a betrayal. And for many of us, that disagreement can create walls in our relationships. Maybe your parents don't understand your career choices. Maybe your partner doesn't get why you're so driven. Or maybe your kids just don't get it—why they need to work harder or prioritize certain things.

When we refuse to respect someone else's worldview, especially in family relationships, it's like we're saying, "You need to see it my way, or I can't connect with you."

And we know that's not true. Let's be real—families are complicated. Everyone's been shaped by their own experiences, and those experiences may have led them to conclusions or lifestyles that we don't agree with. But just because we don't agree doesn't mean we shouldn't respect their right to have their perspective.

What Respect Is—and What It's Not

Let's take a moment to unpack what respect actually means. Respect doesn't mean agreement. It doesn't mean liking or adopting someone else's beliefs. And it definitely doesn't mean tolerating behavior that crosses your boundaries.

Respect is about acknowledgment. It's saying, "I see that your perspective is valid for you." It's recognizing that their worldview—shaped by their experiences, culture, and choices—makes sense to them, just like yours makes sense to you.

But respect also has limits. It doesn't mean giving someone a free pass to hurt you or impose their beliefs on you. You can respect someone's worldview while firmly saying, "That doesn't work for me."

Meet Charles

Charles could feel his life unraveling, one strained relationship at a time. A 48-year-old financial consultant, Charles had built a career—and a reputation—on being sharp, decisive, and unyielding. In his professional world, those qualities were celebrated. But at home? They were slowly tearing everything apart.

His wife, Sarah, had recently asked for a trial separation. She said she needed "space to breathe" which Charles interpreted as her giving up on their marriage. His two teenage daughters barely spoke to him, their once-vivid conversations now replaced by clipped answers and slammed doors. Even at work, where he used to command respect effortlessly, he noticed an edge in his team's responses—a hesitance to engage, as though they were tiptoeing around him.

Charles couldn't understand it. To him, he was doing everything right. He worked hard, provided for his family, and made decisions that were logical and sound. Yet somehow, everyone seemed to be turning against him. In his mind, they were the problem. "I'm holding things together," he thought. "And they're treating me like the enemy."

When Charles came to me, he wasn't looking for answers—he was looking for validation. He wanted me to tell him he was right, that the world around him had gone soft, and that his way of thinking was the solution, not the problem.

"I've done everything for them," he said during our first session, his frustration spilling over. "I've given them a good life, structure, and discipline. And now they act like I'm the bad guy. Sarah says I don't listen, but I do listen—I just know what's best. The girls? They don't even respect me anymore. Everything has to be their way, and when I try to guide them, I'm the villain."

As he spoke, a pattern began to emerge. Charles wasn't just frustrated—he was hurt. Beneath the surface of his defiance was a man who felt deeply unappreciated and misunderstood. But instead of confronting that pain, he doubled down on his beliefs. In his eyes, admitting he might be part of the problem felt like losing everything he'd worked so hard to build—his authority, his credibility, his identity.

Charles's rigidity wasn't just about being right—it was about survival. If he could keep control, if he could convince everyone to see things his way, he wouldn't have to face the uncertainty of stepping into someone else's shoes. He wouldn't have to confront the possibility that his need to be right was driving the people he loved the most further away.

Charles didn't see any of that yet. To him, he was the victim in this story—a man who had done his best, only to be met with resistance and rejection.

Does any of this sound familiar? Maybe you've felt like Charles—frustrated that no one seems to understand your perspective, exhausted from carrying the weight of being "the one who knows best." Or maybe you've been on the other side, trying to connect with someone whose need to be right creates a wall between you.

Wherever you find yourself, one thing is clear, holding onto your perspective at the expense of others doesn't create the peace you're looking for. It creates conflict, isolation, and a cycle of frustration that keeps everyone stuck.

So, how do we break the cycle? By stepping back and exploring the deeper beliefs, fears, and desires driving this need for control. As Charles would soon discover, loosening his grip on being right wasn't about losing himself—it was about finding the emotional freedom and connection he'd been searching for all along.

Where the Need to Be Right Began

As Charles and I began our coaching sessions, it became clear that his frustration wasn't just about the present—it ran much deeper. I could sense there was something beneath his rigidity, something that had been with him long before his wife, his kids, or his business struggles.

"Charles," I asked one day, leaning forward, "why do you think it's so important for you to always be right? Where does that need come from?"

He hesitated, crossing his arms as if to shield himself from the question. "I don't think it's about being right," he said finally. "I just... I know what works. I've been through enough to know what's best."

I let the silence sit for a moment before gently pressing. "But what happens when someone else sees it differently? Why does that feel so personal to you?"

He shifted uncomfortably in his chair. "I guess I've never thought about it that way," he admitted. "But... I don't know. Maybe it's just how I was raised."

"Tell me about that," I said. "What was it like for you growing up?"

Charles took a deep breath, and for the first time, his posture softened. "My dad... he was a tough man," he said slowly. "He worked hard—two jobs most of the time—and he didn't have a lot of patience for mistakes. If you did something wrong, you'd hear about it. And not in a gentle way."

I nodded, encouraging him to continue.

"He wasn't abusive or anything," Charles said quickly, as if to defend his father. "But he had this way of making you feel... small. Like if you didn't measure up, you weren't worth his time. So, I learned to get things right. I figured out what he wanted, what would keep me out of trouble, and I stuck to that."

"And your mom?" I asked.

"She was the peacekeeper," he said with a faint smile. "Always trying to smooth things over, make sure everyone was okay. But even she would say, 'You know how your father is.' She'd tell me to just do what he wanted, to keep the peace."

As Charles spoke, a picture began to form. His need to be right wasn't about ego—it was a survival mechanism. Growing up, being right wasn't just a preference; it was a way to avoid conflict, to earn respect, and to feel like he mattered.

"When I got something right," he continued, "my dad would actually acknowledge me. Maybe he'd say, 'Good job,' or maybe he'd just stop criticizing me for a while. Either way, it felt like a win. So, I guess I just kept chasing that."

"And how did that play out as you got older?" I asked.

Charles paused, looking down at his hands. "I guess it became my way of proving myself," he said. "At work, at home... if I could show that I was right, that I knew what I was doing, it felt like I was... enough."

"Charles," I said gently, "do you think that's still true? That being right is what makes you enough?"

He looked at me, startled by the question. "I... I don't know," he said after a moment. "It's just... it's what I've always done."

I nodded. "And how does that feel now? Carrying that weight, always needing to prove yourself?"

He let out a heavy sigh. "Exhausting," he admitted. "And lonely. It's like... no matter how hard I try, it's never enough. My wife says I don't listen, my kids say I don't get it, and my employees... they're just waiting for me to be wrong. I feel like I'm losing everything because I'm doing what I thought I was supposed to do."

As we continued to dig into his story, Charles began to see the pattern. His father's approval *seemed* conditional, and as a child, Charles made that mean that being right was the way to earn love and respect. That belief had driven him for decades, shaping how he showed up in every area of his life.

But now, that same belief was pushing people away. His wife didn't want a husband who always had to be right—she wanted a partner who would listen, who would meet her halfway. His kids didn't need a father who dictated their lives—they needed someone who could respect their choices, even when they were different from his own. And his employees didn't want a boss who shut down their ideas—they wanted a leader who valued their perspectives.

"Charles," I said, "what if being right isn't what your family and team need from you? What if they need you to just... see them?"

He looked at me, his eyes filled with uncertainty. "I don't know how to do that," he said quietly.

And that's where the real work began.

The Cost of Your Commitment to Being Right

Why is it so important for you to be right all the time? No, seriously—what's the payoff? Is it about winning? Proving your intelligence? Or is it about something deeper, something you might not even realize is driving you? Because let's be honest, it's not just about the argument at hand. It never is. The need to be right is tied to something much bigger—and the cost of holding onto it is higher than you might think.

If you're committed to being right, there's likely a part of you that equates being right with being worthy. Somewhere along the way, you might've learned that your value is tied to your competence, to always having the answers, to never being questioned. Maybe it started in childhood when being "good" meant being right—following the rules, getting good grades, doing what you were told. Back then, being right earned you approval, praise, and even love.

As adults, we don't outgrow those patterns just because we leave the playground or the classroom. That need to be right often follows us into our relationships, our careers, our parenting, our friendships. It becomes less about the actual conversation or disagreement and more about protecting the belief, *"if I'm not right, then what am I?"*

For Charles, his commitment to being right wasn't just about winning arguments. It was about preserving an identity he'd built over decades—an identity that said, *"I'm the guy who knows how the world works."* To admit he might be wrong felt like admitting he'd been fooling himself. And that was terrifying.

What about you? What does being right protect for you? Is it your confidence? Your sense of control? Your belief that you've got it all figured out? And what would happen if you let go of it? Does the thought of not being right make you feel small? Invisible? Uncertain? That's the deeper fear—and it's worth looking at.

Let's talk about what this need to be right is actually costing you. Because it's not just about the relationships you're straining or the opportunities you're missing—it's about the emotional toll it takes on you every single day.

When you're committed to being right, you're constantly on guard. Every conversation feels like a potential battlefield where you have to defend your position. Every disagreement feels like a threat to your identity. That's exhausting. You're carrying the weight of needing to prove yourself, and let's be real, it's heavy.

And here's the thing, the more you hold onto being right, the lonelier and more isolated you become. People stop engaging with you—not because they don't care, but because they feel like there's no room for them in the conversation. They're not fighting you because they're stubborn; they're stepping back because they feel dismissed. And deep down, you know it.

Think about your own life. How often have you walked away from a conversation feeling frustrated, replaying the argument in your head, crafting the perfect comeback you didn't say? How often have you lost sleep because you couldn't let go of the need to prove your point? That's the emotional cost—and it's robbing you of peace.

Let's be honest, being right doesn't actually make you happier. It doesn't make you wiser. It doesn't even make you more respected. What it does is close you off—from new ideas, from growth, from connection. When you're so focused on being right, you stop being curious. You stop listening. You stop learning.

The world is full of perspectives, billions of them. And no matter how smart or experienced or accomplished you are, you can only ever see the world through your own lens. When you insist that your way is the only way, you're not just limiting others—you're limiting yourself. You're cutting yourself off from the richness of other viewpoints, the creativity that comes from collaboration, and the peace that comes from knowing you don't have to have all the answers.

For Charles, his need to be right kept him trapped in a rigid way of thinking. At work, his employees stopped sharing ideas because they knew he wouldn't listen. At home, his daughters stopped opening up because they felt dismissed. His relationships weren't strained because he was wrong—they were strained because he couldn't make space for anyone else to be right.

What about you? How often do you shut down someone else's perspective because it doesn't align with yours? How often do you miss the opportunity to grow because you're too busy defending your position? That's the cost—and it's a high one.

Here's the hardest part to admit, the need to be right is often rooted in self-righteousness. It's the belief that your way of seeing the world is the "correct" way, that your experiences and values are the gold standard. But self-righteousness doesn't build bridges—it burns them. It puts you on a pedestal, but that pedestal isn't a place of power. It's a place of isolation.

Charles believed that his values and experiences gave him a better perspective than his wife, his daughters, even his colleagues. But that belief didn't make him stronger—it made him unreachable. And the more he insisted on being right, the more he pushed people away.

So, ask yourself, are you holding onto being right because you truly believe it will make things better? Or are you holding onto it because you're afraid of what happens if you let go? Truthfully, self-righteousness doesn't protect you—it traps you. And the longer you hold onto it, the harder it is to break free.

What This Means for You

This isn't just about Charles—it's about you. If you're feeling stuck in your relationships, if you're carrying tension or frustration, if you're constantly replaying arguments in your mind, ask yourself, is your commitment to being right worth the cost?

The reality is, being right doesn't make you better. It doesn't make you more valuable. And it definitely doesn't make you happier. What it does is keep you locked in a cycle of defensiveness and frustration, closing you off from the very things you want most—peace, connection, and freedom.

So, why is it so important for you to be right all the time? And more importantly, what are you willing to lose for it? Because if being right means losing the people who matter most, is it really worth it?

The Mental Prison of Black-and-White Thinking

Let me tell you a story I once heard. It's about a Russian kid who came from a long line of chess grandmasters. His family had spent generations perfecting their strategies, passing down secrets from parent to child, like sacred heirlooms. To them, chess was more than a game—it was a way of life, a source of pride, and proof of their brilliance.

This kid had been taught the rules, the strategies, and the moves that had won championships for decades. He was the best player his family had ever produced, a prodigy trained by the best of the best. Then, one day, someone had the bright idea to pit him against a chess-playing AI.

The result? The AI wiped the floor with him. Over and over again, the kid lost. It wasn't even close.

Why? Because while the kid's strategies had been honed and perfected over generations, the AI had no such limits. It wasn't bound by, *"this is how it's always been done"*. It didn't cling to the rules and patterns the way the kid did. The AI could see possibilities the kid's family had never considered because they were trapped in their own brilliance. Their success had become a set of walls, boxing in their thinking and shutting out creativity.

Here's the punchline: the very thing that made the kid great—his reliance on those tried-and-true strategies—was the same thing that held him back. And isn't that how most of us live? The beliefs and rules we cling to for safety and success are often the same things that keep us stuck.

Imagine you're floating in the middle of a vast ocean. The waves are crashing, the water is wild, and you're clinging to a buoy like your life depends on it. That buoy represents your beliefs—the things you're absolutely certain about, the things you think are keeping you safe.

The buoy feels solid, dependable, and comforting. But here's the problem, it's also keeping you stuck. You can't move forward while you're clinging to it. You're holding on so tightly that you don't even notice the freedom of the open water around you.

And then, just like in the chess story, something comes along to challenge you. Maybe it's a person with a completely different perspective. Maybe it's a life event that doesn't fit neatly into your black-and-white worldview. Or maybe, like Charles, it's your relationships crumbling under the weight of your rigidity. Whatever it is, it feels like the waves are getting rougher, and your grip on the buoy tightens.

That's when I show up, riding on the deck of a Disney cruise ship. I'm waving at you, shouting, "Hey! Let go of the buoy and swim over here. There's a whole world of freedom, joy and peace waiting for you. But you have to let go first."

And what happens? You hesitate. The water looks deep, the waves feel scary, and even though the cruise ship is right there, you're afraid. What if you let go and drown? What if you can't make it to the boat? What if the buoy really is your only lifeline? So, you stay put, gripping tighter, convincing yourself that staying stuck is safer than taking the leap.

What you aren't seeing is the water is so dense and salty that you can't actually drown. But you don't know that because you're so focused on clinging to what you think is keeping you safe. And the cruise ship? It's not just about joy and freedom—it's about possibility. It's about stepping into a life where you're no longer bound by the limits of your beliefs.

This is what black-and-white thinking does. It convinces you that the world is simple: right or wrong, good or bad, success or failure. It tells you that your way of seeing things is the only way. It promises you certainty, but at what cost? Certainty, my friend, is the enemy of growth.

When you live in black-and-white thinking, you close yourself off to the endless possibilities that life offers. You can't see the gray areas, the nuances, the "what-ifs" that could change everything. Instead, you're stuck, clinging to your buoy, fighting against the waves, when the ocean itself is trying to show you something new.

Those beliefs you cling to? They feel safe because they're familiar. But safety and growth don't live in the same house. The more you cling to your beliefs, the more they turn into a prison. And the worst part is, it's a prison you don't even realize you're in.

Think about Charles. His black-and-white thinking wasn't just about being right—it was about control. He thought his beliefs were protecting him, but they were actually isolating him. They were pushing away his wife and daughters, alienating his team at work, and creating a life of tension and frustration.

When we dug into his story, Charles began to see how his beliefs were limiting him. He realized that his commitment to being right wasn't just about his own values—it was about fear. Fear of being vulnerable. Fear of losing control. Fear of stepping into the gray areas where he didn't have all the answers.

Peace Lies in the Gray

Now let me ask you, what beliefs are you clinging to? What "rules" have you built your life around that might actually be holding you back? Are you so committed to being right that you've stopped being open? Are you so afraid of the unknown that you're willing to trade freedom for familiarity?

Life isn't black and white. It's a spectrum of colors, a kaleidoscope of experiences, and the moment you let go of the need to define everything in simple terms is the moment you start living. So, here's your challenge, are you ready to stop clinging to the buoy and start trusting the ocean?

That's the thing about life, it's messy. It's nuanced. And it's rarely as simple as black and white. But the human mind? Oh, it loves to label, categorize, and sort everything into neat little boxes– right or wrong, good or bad, success or failure. It makes us feel safe, like we've got it all figured out. But the truth is, life doesn't fit into those tidy categories—and trying to force it to fit only leads to frustration and suffering.

Peace doesn't live in the extremes. It doesn't thrive in the absolutes of "always" or "never." Peace lies in the gray—in the space where two seemingly opposing truths can coexist. It's not about choosing one over the other; it's about finding balance and embracing the complexity of life.

Living in the gray means letting go of the need for certainty and embracing the unknown. It means accepting that you don't have to have all the answers to feel grounded. It's understanding that there's rarely one "right" way to do something or one "right" perspective to have.

Let's say you're in a heated debate with a friend. They're passionate about their point of view, and so are you. Black-and-white thinking says one of you has to be right and the other wrong. Living in the gray says, "What if we're both seeing this through the lens of our own experiences, and neither of us has the full picture?" It's not about winning the argument; it's about understanding that both perspectives hold value—even if they don't align.

Living in the gray is also about releasing the pressure to define everything. Think about how much energy you waste trying to label things, *"This relationship is good,"* or, *"This job is bad."* The gray says, "What if it's both? What if it's neither? What if it's just a moment in time, and it's okay to let it unfold without slapping a label on it?"

So, how do you live in the gray? It starts with a mindset shift. Here are a few ways to step into the gray:

1. **Release the Need to Be Right**
   Ask yourself, "What's more important? Being right, or being connected?" This doesn't mean you abandon your values or beliefs—it means you create space for others' truths to exist alongside yours.
2. **Practice Curiosity Instead of Judgment**
   Instead of immediately dismissing someone else's perspective, get curious. Ask, "Why do you see it this way? What experiences have shaped your view?" Curiosity opens doors; judgment slams them shut.
3. **Embrace Uncertainty**
   Life is full of unknowns, and that's okay. Instead of fearing uncertainty, see it as an opportunity to learn and grow. When you stop demanding answers, you make room for possibilities.
4. **Let Go of Labels**
   Not everything has to be "good" or "bad." The truth is things *just are*. Let yourself experience life without constantly trying to define it.
5. **Hold Multiple Truths**
   Two or more things can be true at the same time. You can love someone deeply and still feel frustrated by them. You can respect someone's perspective and still disagree with it. Peace lies in recognizing that life is rarely either/or—it's usually both/and.

Living in the gray doesn't mean you don't care or that you let people walk all over you. It's not about being indifferent or avoiding hard conversations. In fact, it's the opposite. Peace in the gray requires more engagement, not less. It asks you to stay present, to listen deeply, and to approach every interaction with an open heart and an open mind.

Think of it this way, black-and-white thinking is like building walls to protect yourself. Living in the gray is like planting a garden. It takes effort, patience, and trust, but the result is something far more beautiful and life-giving.

Charles' Life After the Breakthrough

As Charles and I continued to work together, the real breakthrough came when he began to see the stories he had carried from his childhood for what they truly were: misunderstandings.

His father, a man of unyielding discipline and high expectations, had shaped Charles in ways he had never fully examined. As a child, Charles had internalized every sharp word, every disappointed look, as a reflection of his own inadequacy. "If I'm not right," young Charles had thought, "I'm not good enough."

But the truth, as we unraveled it together, was much more complex. His father's rigidity wasn't about Charles. It wasn't about whether he was smart, capable, or worthy. It was about his father's own fears, his struggles to provide, his belief that discipline and control were the only ways to prepare his children for a harsh world.

"It wasn't about me?" Charles asked one day, his voice filled with a mix of relief and grief.

"No, Charles," I said gently. "It was never about you. But as a child, how could you have known that? Children make sense of the world the only way they can—by seeing themselves at the center of it. Your dad's reactions weren't a reflection of your worth. They were a reflection of his fears and beliefs."

This realization hit Charles hard. For decades, he had clung to the belief that being right was the key to love, respect, and safety. It had shaped his identity, driven his decisions, and strained his relationships. But now, he began to see the truth: the rigid thinking that had defined his life wasn't a strength—it was a cage.

As we explored this further, Charles began to let go. Not all at once, but piece by piece. He started to question the beliefs that had once felt so solid, so unquestionable. Did being right really make him worthy? Did controlling every situation really keep him safe? Slowly, he began to loosen his grip.

With this new perspective, Charles started to approach his relationships differently. When Sarah shared her feelings, he resisted the urge to correct her or fix the problem. Instead, he listened, truly listened, for the first time in years. With his daughters, he let go of the need to guide every decision and allowed them the space to grow in their own ways.

Charles began to feel a weight lift—not because he had all the answers, but because he realized he didn't need to. The freedom he had been searching for wasn't in being right. It was in being open.

By the end of our time together, Charles wasn't just a better husband, father, and leader. He was a freer man. He had learned to respect not only the perspectives of others but also his own journey—the mistakes, the misunderstandings, and the growth.

And that respect—for himself and for others—became the foundation for a life of connection and peace. Charles didn't need to have all the answers anymore. He just needed to let go of the belief that he did.

The Shift That Sets You Free

So, how do you let go of this rigid need to be right and the burden it brings? It starts with recognizing what it's costing you and deciding that the cost is simply too high. The weight of always needing to be in control, to have the answers, to be "right"—it's exhausting. And what's worse, it's a lie. No one person can hold all the answers, and clinging to the illusion that you do only creates suffering for yourself and those around you.

The shift is simple, though not always easy—let go. Let go of the need to win every argument, to have every conversation align with your perspective, to dictate the path for those around you. When you release the need to be right, you create space for connection, growth, and peace.

Letting go doesn't mean giving up your values or abandoning your beliefs. It means loosening your grip just enough to allow for possibility, for curiosity, for the richness of other perspectives. It means trusting that your worth isn't tied to how many times you "win" in life.

Charles discovered that freedom isn't about holding tighter—it's about opening up. And you can discover that too. The moment you stop trying to control everything and everyone around you is the moment you start to find peace within yourself.

Respect Is the Path to Freedom

Here's the thing about respect, it's not just something you give to others—it's a gift you give to yourself. When you respect someone else's way of seeing the world, even if you don't agree with it, you're not just acknowledging their humanity—you're reclaiming your own.

Respect says, "I see you. I may not fully understand, but I honor your journey, just as I honor my own." And in that acknowledgment, a bridge is built. Not just between you and the other person, but within yourself. You begin to dismantle the walls of judgment, fear, and control that have kept you locked in a cycle of stress and conflict.

Respecting others' perspectives doesn't weaken your own beliefs. It doesn't mean you're conceding or compromising your values. What it does is free you from the prison of thinking your way is the only way. It opens you up to the richness of life—the connections, the lessons, and the opportunities that only exist when you allow yourself to be open.

As Charles learned, respect isn't just about others. It's about you. It's about finding the peace and emotional freedom that come from releasing the need to be right and embracing the beauty of the gray.

The more you respect the world around you, the more you'll find that the world respects you in return. And in that mutual respect, you'll discover a life filled with more joy, more connection, and more freedom than you ever thought possible.

Reflective Questions

Take some time to reflect:

- What beliefs or perspectives are you clinging to, and how are they limiting your relationships and your peace?

- How often do you find yourself needing to be right? What does being right "give" you—and what does it cost you?
- Think of a recent conflict or disagreement. How might the situation have been different if you had approached it with curiosity instead of judgment?
- What would it look like to respect someone else's worldview, even if you don't agree with it?
- Where in your life are you holding onto control, and what might happen if you let go?
- How can you practice living in the gray—seeing multiple perspectives and embracing the complexity of life?
- What steps can you take today to release the need for certainty and open yourself to connection and freedom?

Chapter 15

The Bridge Between Healing and Wholeness

Take a moment to pause. Breathe. Let's reflect on where you've been and what you've accomplished. Because if you've made it this far, something profound is already happening within you.

You've been through a journey—not just through the pages of this book, but deep into yourself. It hasn't been easy, has it? Digging into old stories, confronting beliefs that once felt like the absolute truth, and letting go of survival patterns you thought you'd always need—it's been hard. But it's also been worth it. You're beginning to feel it, aren't you? That subtle shift. The freedom. The lightness. The possibility. You've started to peel back the layers of fear, guilt, shame, and doubt that have weighed you down for so long, and in their place, you're discovering something incredible: the real you.

But before we move forward, let's take a moment to honor where you've been.

The Power of the Eight Keys: A Foundation for Freedom

Think back to when you first picked up this book. Maybe you were skeptical, maybe curious, or maybe desperate for a way to finally feel free. Whatever brought you here, you've walked through the **Eight Keys** with courage and an open heart. These weren't just words on a page. These keys have asked you to challenge everything you thought you knew about your past, your pain, and yourself.

Let's revisit what these **Eight Keys** have shown you:

1. **It Wasn't About You**: You learned that the actions of others—no matter how hurtful—were never a reflection of your worth. Their pain, not your inadequacy, drove their behavior.

2. **It Had Nothing to Do with You**: The shame you carried wasn't yours to hold. Those moments that shaped you were never about your failures—they were about someone else's.
3. **It Was None of Your Business**: You discovered that carrying the burden of what others thought or believed about you only kept you chained to their story. It was never yours to carry.
4. **Everyone's Doing the Best They Can**: You saw that even the most hurtful actions often came from a place of limitation, not malice. This truth may not erase the pain, but it opened the door to forgiveness.
5. **You Were Loved, Just Not the Way You Wanted**: This one might have been the hardest to hear. Realizing that love was present, even if it wasn't expressed in the way you needed, allowed you to soften the resentment and grief.
6. **There Was a Positive Intent**: You began to understand that every behavior—even the harmful ones—was driven by some kind of positive intent, however misguided.
7. **Judging Yourself by Intent, Others by Action**: This key challenged you to look at how unfairly you've treated yourself, holding yourself to impossible standards while giving others the benefit of the doubt.
8. **Respecting Other People's Reality**: Finally, you learned that freedom comes not from controlling others or making them see the world as you do, but from respecting their way of being, even if you don't understand it.

These keys weren't about justifying what happened to you. They weren't about excusing bad behavior or invalidating your pain. Instead, they were about helping you see the truth beneath the surface—a truth that has set you free.

I Celebrate You

Pause here. Take a deep breath and really let this sink in.

You've done the work.

You've questioned beliefs you held onto for years—decades, even. You've challenged the stories that shaped your identity and begun to dismantle the survival strategies that no longer serve you. That's huge. It's transformative.

Do you feel it? Even if it's subtle, there's a shift happening. A lightness. A sense of clarity. Maybe it's the realization that you don't have to carry everything you've been holding onto. Or maybe it's the quiet knowing that you are enough—right here, right now.

Take a moment to celebrate yourself. Because what you've done is extraordinary.

Now, let's talk about where we're going.

The **Eight Keys** are your foundation—a way to release the past and reconnect with your true self. They've helped you clear the emotional clutter and break free from the stories that kept you stuck. But healing isn't the end of the journey. It's the beginning.

You see, the **Eight Keys** were about letting go of who you're not. What comes next is about stepping into who you are.

It's about discovering the version of you that exists beyond the old stories and survival patterns. The version of you that isn't defined by your past or limited by your fears. The version of you that is already whole, already free, and already enough.

But stepping into that version of yourself requires something deeper. It requires a shift—not just in what you do, but in how you see yourself, your thoughts, and the world around you.

The Journey into Wholeness

In the chapters that follow, we're going to take this work even deeper. We're going to move from healing into living. Here's a glimpse of what's to come:

1. **You Are Not Your Thoughts or Identity** – We'll explore the voice in your head that tells you who you are—and why it's not the real

you. You'll begin to see thoughts for what they are: just passing clouds, not the sky itself.
2. **Becoming Childlike Again** – You'll rediscover the qualities you were born with—joy, curiosity, fearlessness, and unconditional love. These aren't things you need to create; they're already within you, waiting to be uncovered.
3. **Emotional Enlightenment** – This is where everything comes together. We'll explore what it truly means to be free—not just intellectually, but emotionally and energetically. You'll learn how to step beyond the mind and experience the peace that has always been yours.

Each chapter builds on the work you've already done, guiding you to step fully into the freedom, joy, and wholeness that have always been yours.

An Invitation to Go Deeper

What would it look like to live as your true self?

Not the version of you shaped by fear, guilt, or shame. Not the version of you trying to prove, perform, or protect. But the real you—the one who is already whole, already enough, and already free.

This isn't about becoming someone new. It's about remembering who you've always been.

The next chapters are an invitation to do just that. To step into a new way of being. To live from a place of peace, love, and trust—not because you've earned it, but because it's who you are.

So, take another deep breath. Let go of any expectations or doubts about what's ahead. Trust that you're exactly where you're meant to be.

Your journey into wholeness begins now.

Reflective Questions

Take some time to reflect:

- What have the **Eight Keys** revealed to you about your past and your true self?
- How do you feel different now than when you started this journey?
- What excites you about stepping into the next phase of this work?

This is your moment to pause, reflect, and gather strength. The next part of the journey is waiting for you—and I'll be here, guiding you every step of the way.

Chapter 16

You Are Not Your Thoughts or Your Identity

When was the last time you stopped to really listen to the voice in your head? You know, that voice that constantly doubts, judges, and worries? The one that tells you why you're not enough, why things never work out, or what you should've done differently?

Most of us spend our entire lives listening to that voice, assuming it's *us*. We don't question it because it's been there for so long, it feels like part of who we are. But let me tell you something that could change your life.

That voice? It's not you.

You are not your thoughts.

Take a moment to let that sink in. The voice in your head—the one that criticizes you, second-guesses you, or makes you feel small—is not who you are.

The Water Fast

For years, I'd heard whispers about the benefits of fasting. My friend Tommy, a relentless advocate, had been nudging me for what felt like an eternity. "You've got to try a water fast," he'd say. "It's not just about the physical—it'll open you up spiritually." I'd nod politely, but deep down, the idea held no appeal. The thought of going without food for five days? Torture, plain and simple. Spiritual practices like fasting and meditation weren't on my radar. Honestly, I thought they were for other people—the ones sitting cross-legged on mountaintops or burning sage in their living rooms.

But then something changed.

My wife and I were in Hawaii, soaking in the beauty of paradise, when I felt it—a download from Spirit. It wasn't a voice, not in the way you hear someone speaking, but more of a knowing, a nudge from somewhere deep inside.

"You need to do a water fast," it said, "and start meditating."

The message didn't come with reasons or explanations; it was just there, undeniable and clear. It didn't make logical sense, but it felt like truth.

When we returned home, I couldn't shake the feeling. So, I committed. Five days. No food. Just water.

The first two days were manageable, but by day three, things got intense. My body was screaming at me, "You need to eat!" My mind was even louder, throwing every excuse at me. "This is ridiculous. Just quit already. What's the point?" It felt like an all-out rebellion—my body and mind teaming up against me.

But in the midst of that chaos, something extraordinary happened.

A third voice emerged. Not a voice exactly—more like a presence. It wasn't frantic like my mind or desperate like my body. It was calm, steady, and quiet. And it said, *calm down*.

It wasn't a suggestion. It wasn't pleading. It was simply, truth. And in that moment, I realized something profound. I was watching my thoughts. I was observing my body's tantrum, my mind's chatter. If I was observing them, I couldn't be them.

This wasn't just a passing thought—it was an experience that shook me to my core. It was as though a veil had been lifted, and for the first time, I truly saw myself as I am. A spiritual being, living in a physical body, with a mind as a tool.

For years, I had known this concept intellectually. I could recite it, explain it, even teach it. Bob Proctor's SIP framework—Spiritual, Intellectual, Physical—was etched into my brain. I understood it. We are spiritual beings first, with an intellect to think and a physical body to act. On paper, it was clear and logical.

But there's a difference between knowing something with your mind and experiencing it with your soul.

Before this fast, I thought I "got it." But the truth is, I was still living from the intellect and the physical. My days were consumed with doing, thinking, planning, and reacting. The spiritual part? It was more like a checkbox on a list of things I knew I should prioritize but never really did.

That moment of clarity during the fast changed everything. I didn't just understand SIP anymore—I felt it. I was it. My body's hunger and my mind's resistance were loud, but they weren't *me*. What I truly was—what I truly *am*—is the presence that can observe it all without getting swept away.

And that changed everything.

You Are Not Your Spacesuit

Imagine you were headed to space tomorrow. What would you need? A spacesuit, right? But not just any spacesuit—you'd need one with a built-in computer system to regulate your oxygen, control pressure, and keep your body at the right temperature.

Are you the spacesuit? No.
Are you the computer system running the suit? No.
You're the being inside of it—the one experiencing space, moving through it, deciding what to do next.

This is exactly what it's like to be here, in this human experience. You, at your core, are not the body. You're not the mind either. You are the awareness inside of it all.

Bob Proctor called it **SIP—Spiritual, Intellectual, Physical.** You are first and foremost a **spiritual being**—pure awareness, pure consciousness. Your **intellect** is the computer system running the show, processing information, making decisions, and filtering experiences. And your **physical body** is the suit you're wearing to navigate this reality.

Most people live their entire lives thinking they *are* the suit. Or worse, they think they *are* the programming running inside the suit. They identify so strongly with their thoughts, emotions, and past experiences that they forget they are the one inside all of it.

And that's where suffering happens.

Because if you think you *are* the spacesuit, then every scratch on it, every malfunction, every outdated piece of software running inside the system suddenly feels personal—like it defines you. But it doesn't.

Just like if your spacesuit got a dent while walking on the moon, it wouldn't change who you are.

Living Beyond the Suit

Living from the spiritual doesn't mean rejecting the mind or body. It means recognizing them for what they are and no longer being ruled by them. The mind becomes a sharper tool when it's not burdened by self-doubt and fear. The body moves with more grace and alignment when it's not weighed down by the stress of an overactive mind. And life itself begins to flow in ways you never imagined.

That moment during my fast wasn't just a realization—it was a homecoming. It was the moment I stopped searching outside of myself and started living from the truth of who I am. And let me tell you, once you experience that, there's no going back.

As I sat in the stillness of that water fast, watching my thoughts like an observer in a theater, a question rose within me: *If I'm not these thoughts, then who or what is this voice?*

That voice—the one that had been screaming for me to eat, shouting that this fast was ridiculous—wasn't new to me. It had always been there, narrating my life with a mix of judgment, fear, and doubt. But for the first time, I saw it for what it truly was: not *me,* but a product of my mind.

You see, that voice is a mix of old beliefs, past experiences, and survival strategies we've developed over time. It's like a running commentary, trying to make sense of the world and keep us safe. It's our mind's way of navigating life, but the problem is that the mind's idea of "safe" is often rooted in fear.

Let me explain.

Think back to your childhood. Maybe someone told you that you weren't smart enough, or lovable enough, or good enough. Maybe you had experiences that reinforced those beliefs, and over time, your mind built stories around them. It held onto those stories because it thought they'd protect you. *If I believe I'm not good enough, maybe I won't take risks and get hurt. If I stay small, I'll stay safe.*

That voice isn't you. It's just a conditioned pattern—an echo of the past trying to shape your present. It pulls from what you were told, from the wounds you've carried, and uses them to create filters for how you see the world.

During that fast, I realized that my mind wasn't trying to harm me—it was trying to help, in its own distorted way. It was replaying old fears and doubts, not because they were true, but because it thought they'd keep me from getting hurt. But instead of keeping me safe, those thoughts had become a prison.

The voice isn't the enemy; it's just misunderstood. It's not malicious—it's just doing what it's been programmed to do. But the most profound realization I had was this: the voice isn't *me*.

The real me—the real *you*—is the one who notices the voice. It's the awareness that watches the mind's chatter without getting swept away by it. That awareness is your true essence. It's steady, unchanging, and limitless, like the sky.

Why This Matters

By the fourth day of my water fast, I had this profound realization: *I am not my thoughts*. It felt liberating, but I knew this wasn't just some abstract idea to tuck away—it mattered in a deeply practical way. Why? Because for years, I had been living as if those thoughts were *me*.

Believing that voice in your head is who you are is what keeps you stuck. It's what kept *me* stuck—doubting myself, feeling small, chasing validation, or striving for some external achievement to drown out the noise. I'd wake up every morning, and the first thing I'd hear wasn't the birds outside or the sound of my breath. It was the voice. It would say things like, *"What if you're not good enough? What if you fail?"*

That voice isn't neutral. It shapes how you see yourself, how you interact with others, and how you experience the world. I saw this so clearly during the fast. When my mind shouted, *"You need to eat! You can't do this!"* my body felt weak, heavy, like I couldn't take another step. But when I chose to trust the calm, steady presence within me—that part that said, *"Keep going, you've got this"*—everything shifted. I felt lighter, stronger, clearer.

Here's why that happens, your thoughts don't just describe your experience—they create it.

If you wake up thinking, *"Today's going to be awful,"* your mind will find proof to confirm that. It's like putting on tinted glasses that filter out everything good. But if you wake up thinking, *"I trust today to unfold exactly as it should,"* you'll start noticing the small, beautiful moments you might have missed. A kind smile from a stranger, the way the sunlight dances through the trees, or the unexpected ease of a task you thought would be difficult.

Thoughts Are Not Reality

The key is understanding this, while thoughts shape your experience of reality, they are not reality itself. They are interpretations—stories your mind tells to make sense of the world. And like any story, you have the power to question them, rewrite them, or let them go.

This is what Jesus meant when he said, "You will know the truth, and the truth will set you free" (John 8:32). He wasn't talking about memorizing facts or doctrines. He was pointing to something much deeper—the truth of who you are beneath the noise of your thoughts.

During that fast, I caught a glimpse of this truth. I saw that the voice in my head wasn't me, and that I didn't have to believe every story it told. It felt like stepping out of a cage I hadn't even realized I was in. For the first time, I wasn't at the mercy of every critical thought or fearful projection. I could simply watch them, like clouds passing in the sky.

A Shift in Perspective

When you begin to see this, even for a moment, something shifts. You realize you don't have to believe every thought that pops into your head. You don't have to let those thoughts control you. You can choose to let them come and go, without attaching to them.

I remember sitting there on the fifth day of the fast, watching my thoughts like I was watching a movie. The fear and doubt were still there, but they didn't feel personal anymore. They were just passing clouds. And beneath them, I could feel something steady, unshakable—the real me. That's what Jesus was pointing to—the truth that sets you free.

This is the truth I want you to see for yourself: *You are not the voice in your head. You are the one who notices the voice.*

Thoughts Are Like Clouds in the Sky

By the fifth day of my water fast, I felt like I had entered a whole new dimension of awareness. That calm, steady presence within me—the one I had discovered when my mind and body were screaming—became my anchor. It was as though I had stepped back from the chaos of my thoughts and could finally see them for what they were: passing phenomena, not truths. And one of the clearest metaphors that came to me during this time was that of the sky and the clouds.

The sky is vast, open, and steady. Clouds drift across it—some light and fluffy, others dark and stormy. But no matter what the clouds look like, the sky itself doesn't change. It doesn't get tangled up in the storm or cling to the sunshine. It simply holds space for it all.

That's exactly what I realized about myself during the fast. My thoughts—the fear, the doubt, the judgments—were like those clouds. They came and went, shifting and changing, but they didn't define me. Beneath all of it, I was the steady, unshakable sky. And just like those clouds, our thoughts about other people—and how they see us—are shaped by fleeting moments, not the whole truth.

We Only Know What We Think About People

You don't see people. You see your thoughts about them.

Think about it—when every interaction you have with someone is the same, you start to box them in. If the only time you talk to your child is to correct them, they start seeing you as the disciplinarian. Not the one who tucks them in at night. Not the one who hugs them when they're scared. Just the one who tells them what they're doing wrong.

And it works both ways. You start seeing them as the one who always needs correcting.

But is that who they really are? Or is that just the version of them you've created in your mind?

It's the same with everyone in your life. You know the "serious coworker" who never smiles? You'd probably be shocked to see them dancing at a wedding or playing with their kids at the park. It's not that they changed—it's that your view of them is based on one snapshot, one context, one experience.

And the truth is, that's all you ever see—snapshots. Glimpses. Little pieces of a whole person.

I don't even know who my wife really is.

I know who she is with me. I know how she shows up in our conversations, our routines, and our shared moments. But I don't know who she is with her friends. I don't know who she is when she's out in the world without me. The same way she doesn't really know who I am outside of what I show her.

We're all walking around experiencing other people through our own filters—our moods, our judgments, our past experiences. We think we're seeing them, but we're really just seeing our thoughts about them.

And they're doing the same thing to us. This is why what someone thinks about you has nothing to do with you. They're not responding to who you are—they're responding to what's going on in their own head:

- How they're feeling in that moment.
- What kind of day they've had.
- Their fears, insecurities, and assumptions.

You could walk into a room radiating confidence and someone might still see you as intimidating—not because of who you are, but because of how they feel about themselves.

You can try to act a certain way, hoping they'll see you differently. But you can't control what's happening in their world—what arguments they had earlier, what memories they're carrying, what beliefs they've already formed about people like you. And that's why it's a waste of energy to worry about it

Here's what's wild—when someone judges you, they're not actually seeing you. They're holding up a mirror.

If they think you're arrogant, maybe it's because they're insecure. If they think you're inspiring, maybe it's because they're craving growth. If they think you're too quiet, maybe it's because they're uncomfortable with silence.

And the same thing happens when you judge someone else. When you call someone cold or distant, is that who they really are? Or is it just the story you've created based on how *you* experienced them?

You don't know them. You only know your thoughts about them. And that's not the same thing.

The Freedom of Letting Go

So, what do you do with this? You stop trying to control how people see you. You stop boxing yourself in. You stop shrinking to fit someone else's story about you. And you stop boxing *them* in too.

Let people be all the different versions of themselves. Let yourself be all the different versions of you. Be serious and silly. Be the provider and the dreamer. Be the disciplinarian and the nurturer.

Because the moment you stop trying to manage perceptions and start focusing on showing up fully, you set yourself free.

The people who are meant to see you will see you. And the ones who don't? That's their story—not yours. When you stop trying to control how others see you, it's like stepping above the clouds.

The Illusion of Identity

At the end of the day, this is what Chapter 16 has been leading up to.

You are not who people think you are. You are not even who *you* think you are. You are the awareness underneath all those labels. You are not the disciplinarian. You are not the provider. You are not the fun one, or the serious one, or any other box someone tries to put you in.

You're the one watching it all. And when you see that—when you stop identifying with the roles and labels—you start to experience freedom. Not the kind of freedom that comes from proving yourself to the world, but the kind that comes from knowing you don't have to. Because you were never those labels to begin with.

Rising Above the Storm

I remember thinking about this metaphor on a flight I took shortly after that fast. It was one of those days when the sky seemed heavy with gray clouds. Everything felt muted, almost oppressive. But as the plane climbed higher, something incredible happened. We rose above the clouds, and suddenly, the world opened up. The sky was bright, endless, and blue. That heavy overcast from the ground? It was just a layer of clouds hiding the reality above.

That's when it struck me, *that blue sky had been there the whole time.* It wasn't gone because of the clouds—it was simply blocked. And that's how it is with your true self. Beneath the storms of your mind—the worry, the fear, the overthinking—you are still there, perfect, whole and untouched. You've been the sky all along.

The thing about storms is they don't last forever. Think about the last time you felt overwhelmed by worry. Did the worry last forever, or did it eventually pass? Every storm does. But the problem is, when we identify with our thoughts, it's like grabbing hold of a cloud and refusing to let go. We try to control the storm, fix it, or outrun it, but that only keeps us stuck in the turbulence.

During my fast, I saw this pattern in myself. My mind would conjure up a storm—thoughts like, *"You can't do this,"* or, *"You're going to fail."* In the past, I would have tried to argue with those thoughts, fight them, or drown them out with distractions. But this time, I just watched. I let them come and go, without attaching to them. And you know what happened? The storm passed.

That's the truth I want you to understand. The storm doesn't need you to fix it—it needs you to let it pass. The real you, the awareness watching it all, is untouched by the storm. It's always been there, steady and infinite, like the sky.

But what happens when you've been living as the storm for so long that you've forgotten you're the sky? When the role you've played to survive becomes so ingrained that you can't tell where it ends and the real you begins?

The Undercover Cop with No Handler

I often say to my clients, "I can't wait to meet the real you." They usually look at me like I'm crazy and respond, "What do you mean? This is me." And that's when I tell them, "No, this is the version of you that was created to survive your environment. You've been playing this role for so long, you've forgotten who you really are."

It's like being an undercover cop with no handler. Imagine going undercover to infiltrate a world that's not your own. At first, you know it's just a role you're playing—a job to be done. But what happens when there's no one to remind you of your true identity? Over time, you start believing you are the role. You forget who you were before the mission began.

That's exactly what happened to me. For years, I played the role of "Steve Bacon," the perfectionist, the people-pleaser, the man always striving to prove his worth. These were survival strategies I had developed as a child to navigate a world where I didn't feel safe or seen. They worked back then—they kept me alive. But as I grew older, those same strategies became the very prison that kept me stuck.

During my awakening, I saw how deeply I had identified with those roles. "Steve Bacon" wasn't real—he was a persona shaped by the stories I told myself and the beliefs I adopted to protect myself. The real me was the awareness underneath it all, the unconditioned presence that had been watching the role play out.

The problem with survival strategies is that they're excellent at keeping you safe but terrible at helping you thrive. They convince you that you need to keep performing, keep proving, keep striving. But that's not who you are—it's just a role you've outgrown.

The **Eight Keys** showed me how to shed those roles and reconnect with my true self. Now it's your turn. It's time to step out of the costume, to let go of the survival strategies that no longer serve you, and to remember the truth of who you are.

Your Natural State Is Already Peace

Peace isn't something you have to create—it's who you already are. Beneath all the noise, beneath every thought that pulls you into worry, doubt, or fear, there is a part of you that has always been still, unshaken, and whole.

Think about it. When you first wake up in the morning, before any thoughts start running through your mind, you're naturally at peace. Nobody wakes up and says, "Damn, I hate that I just woke up." For a brief moment, whether you notice it or not, your mind is still, and you're simply here. That moment is peace.

But then it starts—the thoughts creep in, *"What do I need to get done today? Why did that person say that yesterday? What if this doesn't work out?"* Suddenly, you're thinking your way out of peace, like clouds rolling in to block the blue sky. One of my mentors used to say, "You're just one thought away from being happy, and you're one thought away from being miserable. It's all in your thinking." At the time, I understood that intellectually, but I didn't truly *feel* it—until September 15, 2024 at 11:49 PM.

That night marked a turning point in my life, though it didn't start out feeling like a breakthrough. It was one of the hardest days I can remember. For the first time in over 20 years, I thought about ending it all. The weight of my mind—the constant criticism, doubt, and fear—had become unbearable. Yet, somewhere deep down, I knew not to take that thought seriously. It was just a reflection of my frustration, not a call to action.

I vented to my father over the phone, seeking some kind of relief, but it wasn't enough to quiet the storm inside. Exhausted, I turned on a documentary called *Awakening Mind* and laid on the couch. As I drifted in and out of sleep, I entered that liminal state between wakefulness and dreaming—what some might call the theta state, where the mind is quiet and receptive.

And then, it happened. I heard someone in the documentary say something that pierced through the fog in my mind: *The self can't awaken because awakening is the recognition that there is no self.*

In an instant, I popped up off the couch because something inside me had shifted. It was as if a light switch had been flipped, and I could suddenly see clearly. Steve Bacon—the identity I had clung to for so long—wasn't real. He was just a character, a role I had been playing, shaped by years of conditioning, survival strategies, and the stories I told myself. But *I*—the true I—wasn't Steve. I was the awareness beneath it all, the unconditioned presence watching the story unfold.

For the first time in my life, I experienced what it meant to simply *be*. I went to bed that night with a profound sense of relief, and when I woke up the next morning, my mind was quiet. Completely quiet. It was as though I had been transported to a new reality, one where I didn't need to fight my thoughts or prove my worth. I wasn't trapped in the endless loop of "not enough" anymore. I was free.

In that freedom, I realized something profound. Peace wasn't something I had to chase or achieve. It was already there, waiting for me beneath the storm of my thoughts. It had always been there, like the blue sky hidden behind the clouds. And in that stillness, I found a truth that changed everything: *I wasn't my thoughts. I wasn't Steve. I was nobody—and in being nobody, I was finally free to be everything.*

This awakening wasn't a grand spectacle. There were no clouds parting, no divine figures welcoming me into enlightenment. It was a quiet, unshakable knowing that I didn't have to be the character I had spent my life playing. And in letting go of that character, I returned to my natural state: peace, love, and stillness.

When you understand this—not just with your mind, but with your whole being—you realize that the voice in your head has no power over you. It's just a passing storm, and you are the steady, unchanging sky. The thoughts may come and go, but the real you—the awareness watching those thoughts—remains untouched, infinite, and free.

This is your natural state. This is who you've always been. You've been the sky all along. It's time to remember.

Let me put it another way. Imagine you woke up tomorrow with full-blown amnesia. You didn't remember who you are, where you're from, whether you're married, have kids—none of the details that make up your identity. Yet your body is still here, conscious and alive.

Now here's the question, if you don't remember who you are, who is animating the body? Who is breathing, moving, and experiencing life through this body?

That's the real you—the part of you that exists beyond any identity or story.

If you were your identity, then forgetting who you are would mean you'd cease to exist entirely. But you don't. You still exist, even without those memories or labels.

The truth is, the real you has always been there, quietly observing, untouched by the stories and roles your mind created. Beneath every label, every belief, and every thought, you are a conscious, alive presence.

When you stop identifying with the roles, the stories, and the labels, you realize something profound: You're free. Not free from life, but free to truly live it, to experience it without the weight of who you think you're supposed to be.

You Are Love Itself: The Fullness of Being

After waking up to the truth that I wasn't my thoughts, something even deeper revealed itself to me: I wasn't just free—**I was whole**. In that stillness, in that quiet awareness, I felt a love so complete, so expansive, that it was unmistakable: *This is who I am.*

And this is who you are too.

True authenticity isn't about becoming someone new. It's not about earning approval, checking boxes, or trying to measure up to an idea of who you think you need to be. It's about peeling back the layers of fear, judgment, and self-doubt to uncover the version of yourself that doesn't need to prove anything to anyone. The version of you that simply *is*.

Your true self doesn't need validation. It doesn't need to chase love, recognition, or acceptance from anyone or anything. Why? Because your true self *is* love. It's not something you do. It's not something you give or receive conditionally. It's the very essence of your being.

When I awakened to this truth, my whole perspective on life shifted. For so long, I had been chasing things outside of myself—success, validation, approval—all in the hopes of feeling whole. But the moment I realized I was already complete, the chasing stopped. There was nothing left to seek because everything I was looking for had been within me all along.

This realization doesn't just change how you see yourself—it changes how you move through the world. You stop approaching life from a place of lack, where you're constantly trying to fill a void. Instead, you begin to give from a place of fullness. You don't love others because you're hoping they'll love you back; you love because it's who you are. Love becomes your natural expression, not something you're trying to get.

I remember sitting quietly after my awakening and noticing how everything around me felt lighter. My relationships felt less strained because I no longer needed anyone to make me feel whole. I wasn't looking to my wife, my family, or my work for validation. I didn't need to prove myself anymore. For the first time, I could simply *be*, and in that being, I found the freedom to love without conditions.

When you embody this truth you become a source of love in the world, not a seeker of it. You give—not because you're trying to get something in return, but because giving feels like the most natural thing to do. You radiate love because that's what you are.

This is the power of awakening to your true self. It's not about becoming something more; it's about realizing you've been enough all along. When you let go of the false stories and identities that have been weighing you down, you uncover the boundless love that has always been at your core.

So, what does this mean for you? It means you don't have to keep chasing. You don't have to keep proving. The love, the peace, the wholeness you've been searching for—it's already here, within you. And when you recognize that, everything changes. The need to take from the world disappears, and the desire to give to it becomes your new way of being.

When you stop seeking love and start being it, you become a living reminder to others of what's possible. You show them, not through words but through your presence, that they too are whole, they too are love. And in that way, you become a ripple of transformation in the world, simply by being yourself.

Chapter 17

Becoming Childlike Again

Have you ever noticed how children trust without question? They don't spend their days worrying about bills, deadlines, or whether they'll have food tomorrow. They just are. They move through life with an effortless sense of safety and assurance that everything will work out. It's not something they consciously think about; it's simply how they exist.

I didn't think much about this natural trust as a kid, even though my childhood was far from ordinary. My mom and I bounced between crack houses, homeless shelters, and strangers' couches. We were constantly on the move, yet through all of that, I never felt unsafe. I never doubted that I was cared for.

Looking back, I can't say whether it was a knowing or something beyond words, but I felt guided. Protected. And maybe I was. Because during those chaotic years, I had an "imaginary friend" named Merle.

Merle wasn't the kind of imaginary friend who looked like me or took on a familiar shape. I didn't know what he looked like at all—I just knew he was there. We played games together, and I'd talk to him for hours. If someone tried to sit in an empty chair, I'd protest, "Merle's sitting there!" It was as real to me as anything else in my world.

As I grew up, Merle faded into the background, and life moved on. But years later, in my twenties, I found myself at a convention with thousands of people. It was a massive event, and on the last day, I ran into an odd-looking man in the bathroom. We exchanged pleasantries, nothing more, and went about our day. But as the event wrapped up, I felt a tap on my shoulder. I turned around, and there he was again.

"I have a message for you," he said. I froze. "God says it's time to stop hating Him. He has work for you to do."

I was stunned. My mind was racing. And then I looked down at his name tag.

It said *Merle*.

I can't describe the feeling that washed over me in that moment. It was like everything stopped. The memories of my childhood came rushing back, and for the first time in years, I felt the presence of that childhood trust. I broke down in tears, collapsing into a heap as strangers surrounded me, praying and supporting me.

I didn't understand it at the time. I wasn't spiritual—I was angry with God, bitter about the life I'd lived. But that moment planted a seed. It was as if the universe had been chasing me, reminding me of something I had forgotten: I was never alone. I had never been abandoned.

Years later, after my awakening, I fully understood the lesson that Merle—and my childhood—had been trying to teach me. As kids, we live in the flow of natural trust. We don't worry about how things will work out because, on some level, we just know they will. We are cared for, provided for, and connected to something greater than ourselves.

This is what Jesus meant when He said, "Do not worry about your life, what you will eat or drink; or about your body, what you will wear... Look at the birds of the air; they do not sow or reap or store away in barns, and yet your heavenly Father feeds them," (Matthew 6:25-26).

As adults, we forget this trust. We start worrying about everything—our careers, our families, our futures. We think survival depends on our effort and control. But as a child, you don't strive to survive. You simply live, trusting that everything will be okay.

After my awakening, that trust returned to me. I stopped worrying about how my bills would get paid or how I would provide for my family. I understood that I am not separate from the universe's laws—I am the laws. And when you align with that understanding, you realize there's nothing to fear. Everything is already taken care of.

This is the childlike essence we are called to return to. It's not naive or irresponsible—it's a profound awareness of who you truly are. It's the recognition that you've never been separate from the Source that provides for everything.

Trusting the Voice Within

There's a calm that children possess, one that allows them to face situations that would terrify most adults. It's not something they think about—it just is. It's the kind of trust that says, "*I'm safe, I'm cared for, and I'll be okay.*" I know this because I've experienced it firsthand, even in moments where my safety should have been anything but certain.

When I was about four or five years old, I went with my mom to one of her friends' houses. They had a pool—twelve feet deep. I didn't know how to swim, but that didn't matter. My mom set me on one of those floaties you lay on and turned her attention elsewhere. Maybe she and her friend went inside the house, maybe they were just distracted—I can't say for sure. All I know is that at some point, I shifted on the floaty, and it flipped.

I sank straight to the bottom of the pool.

There I was, a child too young to understand what drowning even meant, standing at the bottom of twelve feet of water. But instead of panic, there was calm. I wasn't thinking about breathing or trying to scream. I just... was.

And then, I heard it: a voice.

It wasn't frantic or loud. It didn't tell me to panic or beg for help. It was steady, clear, and calm. It said, "*Jump.*"

So, I jumped.

Kick, it said.

So, I kicked.

Jump. Kick.

I kept following that voice—jumping, kicking, slowly propelling myself upward. I can still vividly remember looking up at the surface of the water, watching the sunlight dance above me. The voice guided me every step of the way until, finally, my head broke through the surface.

That's when the adults noticed. My mom freaked out, screaming and jumping into the pool to grab me. But by then, I was already safe.

As I think back on that moment now, it's not the danger that stands out to me—it's the peace. There was no fear, no sense of urgency, just a steady, unwavering trust in that voice. At that age, I didn't yet have the filters of doubt, fear, or overthinking that we learn as adults. I simply trusted and acted, and because of that, I survived.

That voice? That's the same inner guidance you have access to, even now. But as we grow older, we stop listening. We let fear and doubt drown it out. We question its wisdom, overanalyze its simplicity, and convince ourselves that we have to figure everything out on our own.

What if you didn't?

What if you could return to that childlike trust, the kind that knows the next step will always reveal itself? What if you stopped fighting the current of life and allowed yourself to be guided by the same voice that told me to jump and kick?

Trust isn't something you need to learn—it's something you need to remember.

Rediscovering Your Original Design

Let's pause for a moment. I want you to think about a brand-new phone—an Apple, a Google, whatever you prefer. Picture that moment you peel back the packaging and hold it in your hand for the first time. It's flawless. It works exactly as its manufacturer intended, capable of incredible things—facilitating connections, creating memories, answering questions and helping you navigate the world. It's perfect, just as it is.

But what happens next? You start adding to it. Photos, notes, apps. Someone sends you a link, and you click it. Maybe that link infects the phone with a virus. Maybe the apps start clogging its memory, slowing it down. One day, the phone that once worked perfectly now barely turns on. It lags. It freezes. You wonder, *"What happened?"*

The thing is, the phone didn't lose its original design. It's still there, under all the junk. It didn't stop being what the manufacturer created it to be. It just got covered up.

You are that phone.

When you came into this world, you were perfect—flawless, unbroken, capable of incredible things. You were naturally joyful, curious, playful, fearless, forgiving, imaginative, and unconditionally loving. You didn't wake up wondering if you were good enough or worrying about tomorrow. You simply *were*.

You didn't have fear because you didn't know fear. You didn't doubt yourself because doubt hadn't been taught to you yet. You didn't seek approval because you instinctively knew you were already enough. That was your original design—the you that existed before society got involved.

But then, the "world" started piling on its programming. When Jesus said, "Be in the world but not of it," he wasn't talking about the Earth itself. He was talking about society—the systems, beliefs, and structures that are designed to keep you small. And it's not just Christianity that speaks to this.

In Buddhism, the term *"samsara"* describes the endless cycle of suffering created by attachment to the illusions of the world. Hinduism teaches us about *"maya,"* the veil of illusion that keeps us from seeing our true selves. The Tao Te Ching reminds us to *"return to the simplicity of an uncarved block,"* meaning the pure, natural state of being we were born with.

Across all these traditions, the message is clear: The world (society) has one job—to distract you, to make you forget who you are. It teaches you fear to keep you controlled. It plants seeds of doubt to make you dependent. It tells you you're not enough so that you'll keep seeking outside of yourself for the answers you already have.

As a child, you didn't know any of this. You lived in alignment with your original design. But as you grew, society started adding layers—conditioning, expectations, fears. Someone told you it wasn't safe to be yourself. Someone else taught you that failure was shameful or that your dreams were unrealistic. Slowly, those layers built up, like junk filling the memory of that perfect phone. And just like the phone, you started to lag. You started to doubt. You started to forget.

Your original design is still there. Just like the phone, you didn't lose your perfection. You didn't stop being the joyful, curious, fearless being you were born to be. All those qualities—the ones you think you have to learn—are already within you. They've just been covered up.

Think back to when you were a child. Remember how fearless you were, how you believed in magic, how the simplest things filled you with wonder. You didn't need a reason to laugh or a strategy to dream big. You simply did. That was your natural state.

And it still is.

The joy, the curiosity, the imagination—they're all still there, waiting for you to rediscover them. They haven't gone anywhere. They've just been buried under layers of fear, doubt, and survival strategies you learned along the way. But those layers aren't who you are. They're not your truth. They're just stories society told you—and you don't have to believe them anymore.

So, let me ask you this, what would it look like for you to peel back those layers? To let go of the fear, the doubt, the need for approval? To reconnect with your original design?

You don't need to become someone new. You don't need to "fix" yourself. **You were never broken**. The perfection you came into this world with is still there, waiting for you to come back to it.

And when you do, everything changes. You start to see life as it really is—a playground, a paradise, a vacation from nothing. You stop chasing and start being. You return to the joy, the love, the wonder that's been with you all along.

Because that's who you are. That's who you've always been.

A Vacation from Nothing

Think about the last time you went on a vacation. Maybe it was a tropical beach, a cozy cabin in the mountains, or even just a long weekend away. For those few days, you probably let go of your usual worries. You didn't think about deadlines, bills, or all the things waiting for you back home. You gave yourself permission to enjoy, to relax, to simply be.

What happened during that time? Chances are, you felt lighter. Your mind slowed down, and you found yourself noticing things you might normally overlook—the way the sun felt on your skin, the sound of birds in the morning, the joy of a good meal. For a brief moment, life felt effortless, peaceful.

Now imagine if that feeling wasn't reserved for vacations. Imagine if you could live like that every day—not because your responsibilities disappeared, but because your relationship with life changed. What if you didn't need a plane ticket or a break from your routine to experience that kind of peace? What if life itself was a vacation?

When you were a child, this was your natural way of being. You didn't worry about tomorrow or try to control what came next. You trusted that everything would be okay because, in your world, it was. Life was a playground, an adventure, a canvas for your imagination. There was no rush, no pressure, no fear—only presence. You lived in the moment, fully immersed in the experience of being alive.

But then, as you grew older, something shifted. The world—society—began teaching you that life was something to manage, to survive, to control. Worrying became a habit. Fear became a motivator. Peace became something you had to chase rather than something you already had.

This is where we lose our way. We start living as if life is a problem to solve rather than a gift to enjoy. Life isn't meant to be a struggle. It's not a test or a punishment or a series of hurdles to overcome. Life is a vacation—a temporary, beautiful experience meant to be explored, savored, and celebrated.

Think about it for a second. Do you really believe this entire universe—this masterpiece of sunsets, oceans, wildflowers, and shooting stars—was created so you could stress over your to-do list? Do you think the same Source that made galaxies thought, "You know what would be great? Watching people obsess over their email inbox and worry about what other people think of them"? Come on. That can't be the point.

Life is a vacation. But here's the thing, vacations don't last forever. You know this. When you book a trip, you don't spend the entire time in your hotel room freaking out about when the vacation will end. No, you dive in. You taste the food, feel the sand under your feet, and let yourself get lost in the moment. That's the whole point.

So why don't we approach life the same way?

Somewhere along the line, we forgot how to let go and enjoy the ride. We got so caught up in deadlines, doubts, and fears that we started treating this gift of existence like a chore. But what if you could let all of that go? What if you stopped replaying every painful moment in your mind like a broken record and started seeing life for what it really is: paradise, here and now.

And I know what you're thinking, "*But life's hard. People hurt me. Bad things happen.*" Yeah, those are possibilities, but the pain you hold onto? That's a choice.

Let's sit with something uncomfortable for a minute: no one can hurt you without your permission. I know, that's a bold statement, but hear me out.

The hurt you feel doesn't come from what someone says or does. It's what happens inside of you. Now, I'm not saying painful moments don't happen. They absolutely can. But how you experience that pain—and whether you carry it with you for the rest of your life—is entirely up to you.

Take a toddler for example. They cry when they fall, right? Or when a toy is taken away. They don't stay hurt. They're not sitting there a week later, holding onto that toy in their mind, plotting revenge. They let it pass. As transformation coach and author Michael Neill puts it, a toddler doesn't need a therapist. They're living proof that our natural state is one of mental health and wellness. Their ability to move past things so easily isn't a learned skill—it's who they are. And it's who you are, too.

So, what happened to you? Somewhere along the way, you learned to hold onto pain. To replay it. To assign meaning to it. The truth is, the pain itself isn't external—it's always an internal experience.

When you become childlike again, you see this for yourself. You remember that no one's words, actions, or opinions have the power to define you unless you let them. You realize the peace inside of you—your joy, your wholeness—is yours to keep. Untouched by anyone else.

A World Designed for Joy

Here's why this perspective matters. Look around you. Really look. This world wasn't created for you to be weighed down by fear and judgment. It was made to be a playground, a canvas, a masterpiece for you to experience fully.

Imagine for a second that you're Source Energy, Infinite Intelligence, God—whatever name you want to give it. You decide to create a world so you can experience life through it. What would be the point of making that world miserable? Would you go to all the trouble of creating flowers, laughter, music, and sunlight just so you could stress over your credit card bill?

No. The purpose would be to live, to play, to explore. To see yourself reflected in every bird, every wave, every star in the sky.

But somewhere along the line, society convinced you otherwise. It taught you that life is hard, that suffering is noble, that joy is fleeting. It convinced you that you have to earn happiness, that you're not enough, that you need to fight for your place in the world.

And you believed it.

Yet, the paradise you're looking for? It's right here. Always has been. You don't have to book a flight to find it. You don't have to wait for retirement or for everything in your life to be "perfect." The perfection is already here.

It's in the way the sunlight filters through the leaves. It's in the sound of children laughing. It's in the rhythm of your own breath, the miracle of being alive.

The only thing keeping you from seeing it is the lens you've been looking through. You've been so busy fighting, striving, and protecting yourself that you forgot to actually live.

The good news is, you can change that. Right now. You can let your guard down. You can let go of the pain and the fear and the endless stories in your head. You can decide to see life the way a child sees it—with wonder, curiosity, and trust.

Because life isn't a problem to solve. It's a vacation to enjoy.

Surrender: The Key to the Kingdom

Let me ask you something—when was the last time you truly let go? I'm not talking about "taking it easy" or "relaxing for a bit." I mean letting go of everything—the control, the fear, the endless cycle of what-ifs. When did you last trust, fully and completely, that everything in your life would be taken care of?

For me, surrender wasn't something I understood growing up. It wasn't even on my radar as an adult. I thought life was about hustling, controlling, making things happen. And for a long time, that worked for me—or at least I convinced myself it did. But there came a moment when life demanded something different, something deeper.

I'll never forget the day my wife told me she was pregnant. I was in Mexico at the time, on a Zoom call, living the life I had spent over a decade building. Traveling first-class, making six figures, calling the shots—it was the dream I had chased ever since I clawed my way out of my past. But when she told me, my world stopped. It wasn't joy or excitement that hit me—it was fear. A suffocating, chest-tightening fear that whispered, *"Your life as you know it is over."*

You see, I had built my life around one thing: success. Not a family, not stillness, not joy—success. Becoming the top 1%, achieving the kind of wealth and recognition that would silence all the voices of doubt and judgment I'd carried since my childhood. A baby didn't fit into that picture. I didn't know how to let it fit.

For months, I spiraled. My business began to crumble, and I felt like everything I had worked for was slipping through my fingers. I tried to hold it together, but the more I held on, the worse it got. I was drowning—not in responsibilities, but in the fear of losing control. And then one day, on October 31, 2023, something inside of me whispered, *"Stop. Let it all go."*

That whisper wasn't just an idea; it was a knowing. Spirit, Source, God—whatever you want to call it—was telling me to sit down and stop trying to hold it all together. And for the first time in my life, I listened. I let go. I told my wife, her family, and even the world through a Facebook post: *I don't have it all together. I'm broke, I'm scared, and I don't know what's next.*

What happened after that was nothing short of miraculous. Within two hours of making that post, someone paid our rent for the next month. In the following weeks, friends, clients, and even strangers began showing up with resources, support, and love I could never have anticipated. When we held our baby shower, it felt like the whole world showed up. We received everything we needed for our daughter—diapers, clothes, formula, furniture, even the big-ticket items. And for a year, without me trying to control or force anything, everything we needed continued to show up.

That year wasn't about me learning to trust. It was about remembering. Trust isn't something you need to learn—it's something you were born with. As children, we don't question whether we'll be fed, clothed, or loved. We just know. We live in that natural state of trust until the world convinces us otherwise.

Jesus said, "Unless you become like little children, you will never enter the kingdom of heaven." He wasn't talking about a place in the clouds or something you reach after death. He was talking about a state of being—a peace so profound it feels like heaven on Earth. And that peace? It comes when you surrender.

And let's be clear—this isn't about religion. Jesus wasn't talking about joining a church or following a doctrine. He was pointing to something universal, something every spiritual tradition speaks of in its own way. In

Buddhism, the concept of "beginner's mind" invites us to approach life with the openness and wonder of a child, free from preconceptions and judgments. The Tao Te Ching reminds us to "return to the simplicity of an uncarved block," to reconnect with our pure, natural state of being. Hinduism speaks of "Lila," the divine play, where life is meant to be a joyous, creative experience rather than a struggle. Across all traditions, the message is the same: peace comes not from striving, but from surrendering to the flow of life.

Surrender isn't giving up; it's waking up. It's realizing that you're not the one holding the universe together—that's already taken care of. It's stepping out of the driver's seat and letting the infinite intelligence that created you take the wheel. And yes, it's terrifying at first. Your ego will scream, *"What about the bills? The deadlines? What will people think?"* But underneath all of that fear is the truth: you were never meant to carry it all. You're not here to micromanage life. You're here to live it.

I want to ask you something, what would happen if you let go? If you stopped trying to control every outcome, every conversation, every possibility? What would happen if, just for a moment, you surrendered and trusted that everything you need is already being taken care of?

I'm not saying it's easy. It wasn't easy for me. But the peace I've found on the other side of surrender? It's worth every ounce of fear I had to let go of. And the same peace is available to you. It's not reserved for the spiritual elite or the lucky few. It's your birthright. It's the Kingdom Jesus spoke of—the one that's been inside you all along, just waiting for you to come home.

Surrender isn't something you have to figure out or earn. It's as simple as breathing, as simple as letting go of the need to hold it all together. Because the truth is, you're already being held. Always have been. Always will be.

Surrender isn't the end of the journey. It's the beginning. When you let go of the weight you've been carrying—the fears, the doubts, the need to control—you make room for something incredible to emerge: *joy!* Not the fleeting kind that comes and goes with good news, but the deep, soul-filling joy you were born with. The kind of joy children live in every single day.

When you were a kid, did you need a reason to laugh? Did you need a detailed plan to explore your backyard or imagine a world where you were the hero? Of course not. You didn't overthink it. You didn't second-guess whether you were "good enough" to dream big or worry about how you'd make it happen. You just *did*.

You were curious about everything. The way the stars lit up the night sky. The way water rippled in a puddle. The way the world seemed full of infinite possibilities. You didn't need anyone's permission to dream or play—you just followed what felt right, what felt fun. And somewhere along the way, you stopped.

It wasn't your fault. Society taught you that curiosity is impractical, that dreaming is childish, and that playing is a waste of time. But let me tell you something: *society is wrong.* Curiosity is how you grow. Dreaming is how you create. And playing? Playing is how you experience the fullness of life.

When Jesus said the Kingdom of Heaven belongs to the childlike, He was pointing us to this truth: joy, curiosity, and playfulness are the keys to living in alignment with who you really are. And they've been waiting for you this whole time. They're not lost—they're just buried under layers of "shoulds" and "musts" and "not enoughs."

The good news is that you can peel those layers back. You can reclaim the wonder you were born with. And it starts with one simple question, *what would a child do?*

A child would see the beauty in the mundane. They'd make a game out of folding laundry or turn an ordinary walk into a grand adventure. They'd ask a million questions, not because they need the answers but because they're in awe of the mystery. They'd find joy in the smallest things—a butterfly landing on their finger, the feeling of sand between their toes, the sound of their own laughter.

You can do that too.

Start small. Let yourself wonder about the things you've stopped noticing. Why is the sky blue? How does a tree know how to grow? Give yourself permission to laugh—really laugh—without worrying whether it's "appropriate." Try something new, just for the fun of it. Paint, dance, sing, build something with your hands. Not because it's productive, but because it's joyful. Because it reminds you what it feels like to be alive.

And most importantly, let go of the voice in your head that says, *"You're too old for this"*, or *"You don't have time for this"*, or *"What will people think?"* That's not your truth. That's your ego, trying to keep you small. But you are not small. You are vast. You are infinite. And joy, curiosity, and playfulness are your birthright.

A New Way of Living

Imagine waking up tomorrow with nothing to prove. No one to impress. No fears weighing you down. What would you do? Where would your curiosity take you? What would it feel like to see the world through fresh eyes again?

This isn't about pretending life is perfect. It's not about ignoring responsibilities or pretending pain doesn't exist. It's about choosing to show up differently. It's about letting the child in you—the one who sees magic in everything—take the lead.

Because that child is still there. They've been waiting for you to remember. To remember that life isn't a test to pass or a burden to bear—it's a gift to be savored. It's a playground, a canvas, an adventure. And it's all yours.

So go ahead. Laugh. Dance. Wonder. Trust. Surrender. Play. Live. Not because you have to, but because you *can*. Because that's what it means to become childlike again. And when you do, you'll discover something you may have forgotten: the Kingdom of Heaven—the peace, the joy, the love you've been searching for—was never out there. It's been inside you all along, just waiting for you to come home.

Chapter 18

Emotional Enlightenment

Take a moment and imagine waking up tomorrow morning, feeling completely free. Not free in the way most people imagine—no responsibilities, no obligations—but free in the deepest, most profound sense. Imagine opening your eyes and feeling light, like you've just put down a backpack you've been carrying for years. Inside that backpack? All the anger, sadness, guilt, fear, hurt and shame you've been holding onto. Gone.

You still remember the moments that shaped you—the struggles, the heartbreaks—but those memories no longer feel heavy. They're no longer tangled up with blame, regret, or resentment. They're just…memories now. Like photographs in an album, you can flip through without reliving the pain.

Now, picture stepping into your day and seeing everything—your relationships, your work, your world—with fresh eyes. No longer filtered through the lens of past hurts or future fears. You're not replaying yesterday's frustrations or preloading tomorrow's anxieties. You're simply here, fully present, fully alive.

That's *Emotional Enlightenment.*

It's not about suppressing your emotions or pretending they don't exist. It's about changing your relationship with them. Emotions become like clouds passing through a clear sky—momentary, fleeting, and no longer in control. You're the sky, not the clouds. You experience them, but you don't become them.

And let me be clear, this isn't some mystical, out-of-reach state reserved for monks or gurus on mountaintops. It's real. It's practical. And it's available to you. Right here, right now.

This doesn't happen by accident. It takes work. It takes courage. It takes being willing to open the closet, look at the things you've been afraid to face, and see them with fresh eyes. That's the cost.

And it's worth it.

Because this isn't just about feeling better. This is about freedom. True freedom. The kind of freedom that allows you to walk through life unshaken, rooted in a peace that can't be disturbed by what's happening around you.

And here's the best part—it doesn't take forever. *Emotional Enlightenment* isn't something you have to chase for years or decades. It's not about spending your life in therapy or meditating in a cave. It's about deciding—today—that you're ready to face yourself, to release what's been holding you back, and to step into the freedom that's already waiting for you.

You've been preparing for this moment since the first page of this book. Every key you've unlocked, every belief you've questioned, every piece of emotional weight you've let go of has been leading you here.

So, let's go deeper. Let's explore what this freedom looks like, how it's possible, and what it takes to live from this space—not just for a moment, but as a way of being.

Making It Tangible

Emotional Enlightenment isn't just a lofty idea or an abstract state of being. It's not about reaching some unattainable level of perfection where you never feel anger, sadness, or frustration again. It's about shifting how you experience those emotions when they arise.

Let's define it plainly: *Emotional Enlightenment* is the state of deep self-awareness and emotional clarity where you have transcended the typical constraints of negative emotions such as anger, sadness, fear, hurt, guilt, and shame. It involves understanding and transforming your emotional responses, leading to a more profound sense of inner peace, joy, and unconditional love. It's not about getting rid of emotions or pretending they don't exist—it's about changing your relationship with them. This state often results from practices that promote emotional healing, self-reflection, and personal growth, allowing you to live more authentically and harmoniously.

When you're *Emotionally Enlightened*, emotions become what they were always meant to be: signals. They pass through you like a breeze moving through an open window. You feel them, but they don't define you. They don't control your thoughts, dictate your actions, or shape your identity. You experience them fully, and then you let them go.

Think of it like standing in a thunderstorm. Most of us spend our lives trying to fight the storm—running from the rain, shouting at the clouds, or pretending the storm doesn't exist. *Emotional Enlightenment* is like standing under shelter. The storm still happens, but it doesn't consume you. You can see it for what it is—temporary, passing, and not a reflection of who you are.

This doesn't mean life becomes perfect. Challenges will still come. People will still be people. Unexpected things will still happen. But when you're *Emotionally Enlightened*, those moments don't derail you. They don't pull you into a spiral of anger, fear, or regret. You remain steady, rooted in a peace that comes from within—a peace that can't be taken away by anything outside of you.

Emotional Enlightenment isn't tied to one religion or philosophy—it's a state of being that wisdom traditions around the world have described in their own unique ways. It's like the downtown of a city. No matter where you live, there are countless roads that lead there. Some are scenic and winding; others are direct and straightforward. But they all take you to the same destination.

And that destination? It's the inner stillness and freedom we're talking about here. Strip away the cultural expressions, the rituals, the doctrines, and what's left is the same universal truth: peace isn't something you find out there. It's what you uncover in here, within yourself.

When I think about these roads, I imagine the people who've traveled them. Every path was paved by someone seeking the same thing—a way to transcend the noise, the chaos, and the emotional weight of life. They didn't have identical journeys, but they were all walking toward the same light, the same center.

It's easy to get caught up in the differences—the names, the symbols, the language. But when you take a step back, you'll see that they're all pointing to the same reality. Whether it's described as awakening, liberation, or enlightenment, the essence remains: freedom comes not from controlling the world around you, but from releasing the grip it has on you.

Here's the thing about *Emotional Enlightenment*, it's timeless. It's universal. Again, it's not reserved for saints, gurus, or monks meditating on mountaintops. It's for anyone willing to look within, to step off the beaten path of reactivity and explore what lies beyond. It's not about abandoning the road you're on—it's about recognizing where it's leading and choosing to walk it with greater intention and awareness.

So, think of your own journey. What road have you been on? Has it felt winding, like you're circling the same struggles over and over? Or has it felt like a straight shot, only to realize you've missed the heart of what you were searching for? Wherever you've been, know this: the destination isn't somewhere out there. It's been within you all along.

Emotional Enlightenment isn't something you achieve; it's something you uncover. It's a remembering. It's the realization that beneath the stories, the pain, the struggle, there is a part of you that has always been whole, pure, and at peace. And when you experience that space—when you truly see it for what it is—you'll understand that every step you've taken, every twist and turn, was leading you here.

Here's another way to think about it, imagine a cluttered room. When it's filled with old boxes, broken furniture, and scattered debris, it's hard to see the space for what it really is. You trip over things, feel crowded, and even start to believe that the mess defines the room itself. But when you clear it out—when you remove what doesn't belong—you see the truth. The room isn't the clutter; it's the open, expansive space that was always there underneath.

That's what *Emotional Enlightenment* is. It's not about adding anything new to yourself. It's about clearing away what was never meant to be there in the first place.

And the most beautiful part is, *Emotional Enlightenment* isn't about perfection. It's not about never feeling anger, sadness, or frustration again.

It's about recognizing that you are not your emotions—you're the space they move through.

This is what freedom feels like. It's not an escape from life—it's a new way of living it. It's meeting each moment with presence, clarity, and grace, no matter what's happening around you.

Emotional Enlightenment as a Practice, Not a Destination

If *Emotional Enlightenment* is the downtown of your city—the heart of peace and freedom—then the **Eight Keys** are the roads that bring you here. Each key helps you let go of something heavy, something you didn't even know you were carrying. Together, they clear the way so you can start living from this lighter, freer place.

However, the thing about arriving downtown is that you don't just stop and stay there forever. You still have to navigate the city. Life keeps moving, people keep showing up, and challenges will still find their way to you. The difference is, now you know the way. You have a map, and you've walked the road. That's what *Emotional Enlightenment* is—a practice, not a destination.

Let's be real about this. Anger might flare up when your boundaries are crossed. Sadness might visit when life doesn't go the way you hoped. Fear might whisper to you in moments of uncertainty. The shift is that those emotions won't take you over anymore. They'll show up like guests, stay for a moment, and then leave. They'll stop running the show.

Emotions Are Just Signals

Think of emotions like the warning lights on your car dashboard. When they come on, they're not trying to ruin your drive—they're giving you information. Fear says, "Something feels unsafe." Sadness says, "Something meaningful has been lost." Anger says, "A boundary has been crossed."

When you're emotionally reactive, it's like ignoring those lights or smashing the dashboard in frustration. You're either running on empty or letting the car break down because you didn't pay attention. *Emotional*

Enlightenment changes that. You start to notice the signals without overreacting to them. You respond, but you're no longer controlled by them.

The **Eight Keys** offers these perspectives as a guide:

- **It Wasn't About You** teaches you to see other people's actions for what they are—a reflection of their own struggles, not your worth.
- **It Had Nothing to Do with You** reminds you that the pain you've carried wasn't your fault.
- **It Was None of Your Business** helps you stop carrying the weight of other people's opinions and start living for yourself.
- **Everyone's Doing the Best They Can** softens your resentment by helping you see that even hurtful actions often come from someone else's pain.
- **You Were Loved, Just Not the Way You Wanted** shows you how to release the hurt tied to unmet expectations.
- **There Was a Positive Intent** helps you understand that even harmful behavior came from some misguided attempt to meet a need.
- **Judging Yourself by Intent, Others by Action** challenges you to treat others with the same compassion you've shown yourself.
- **Respecting Other People's Reality** helps you let go of the need to fix or control others and gives you the freedom to focus on yourself.

Each of these keys helps you shift how you see the world, and in doing so, they start to shift how you feel. The anger, fear, sadness, hurt and guilt that once weighed you down don't have the same hold on you anymore. You can acknowledge them without being consumed by them.

Daily Practices to Stay Aligned

Now that you've cleared the path to *Emotional Enlightenment*, the real work begins. And yes, I said work. This is the part most people avoid because it doesn't sound glamorous. But let me tell you something, the most profound transformation isn't just about the big breakthroughs—it's in the small, daily choices that keep you aligned with the peace you've uncovered. This is where *Emotional Enlightenment* becomes less of an event and more of a practice. And like any practice, it takes commitment, consistency, and grace with yourself.

Here's what a daily practice looks like:

1. **Awareness**: When an emotion arises, notice it. Don't push it away or let it take over—just notice. Allow yourself to feel without judgment. Ask yourself, *"What is this emotion trying to tell me? Is it pointing to a boundary that needs to be set? A wound that needs to be healed? Or is it simply a story I've been carrying that no longer serves me? What's the story I'm attaching to this?"*
2. **Release**: The moment you feel an intense emotion rising, pause. Once you've acknowledged the emotion, let it go. Sometimes this is as simple as taking a deep breath and grounding yourself in the present moment or writing it down. Imagine the emotion as a wave passing through you. You don't need to hold onto it. Let it come, let it teach you, and then let it go. Other times, it might mean revisiting one of the **Eight Keys** to untangle what's really happening.
3. **Choice**: You have a choice in every moment. You can cling to the old stories, the old patterns, the old emotions—or you can let them go. Every time you release an emotion, you create space to choose how you respond. You can choose to see life through the lens of fear, anger, and hurt—or you can choose to see it through the lens of peace, love, and possibility. This choice isn't always easy. But every time you make it, you reinforce the freedom you've worked so hard to create. You remind yourself that you are not your emotions—you are the space they move through.

It's a cycle—awareness, release, choice—and the more you do it, the easier it becomes. This practice doesn't end when you finish this book. It's a lifelong journey, one you'll walk every day. And here's the beauty of it: the more you apply it, the lighter you'll feel. Over time, this way of being will feel as natural as breathing. The more you choose freedom, the more natural it will become. And before you know it, this way of being—this state of *Emotional Enlightenment*—will stop feeling like work. It'll just be who you are.

One of the most beautiful things about living from a place of *Emotional Enlightenment* is the impact it has on those around you.

When you show up with clarity, peace, and presence, you give others permission to do the same. Your calm becomes contagious. Your ability to hold space for others without reacting inspires them to explore their own inner freedom.

You don't have to preach or teach. Simply by being an example, you create a ripple effect. You show people what's possible.

Staying in a state of *Emotional Enlightenment* requires intention. Here are a few daily rituals to help you stay aligned:

1. **Morning Reflection:** Start your day by grounding yourself. Spend a few moments in gratitude, reflecting on what you want to carry into your day. This sets the tone for how you'll respond to life's challenges.
2. **Mindful Check-Ins:** Throughout the day, pause to check in with yourself. How are you feeling? What thoughts are running through your mind? Are you reacting from old patterns, or are you responding from a place of clarity?
3. **Evening Release:** Before you go to bed, take a moment to reflect on your day. Is there anything you're holding onto that you need to release? Imagine letting it go, like setting down a heavy bag you no longer need to carry.
4. **Reconnect with the Eight Keys:** The **Eight Keys** aren't just tools for big breakthroughs—they're guides for everyday life. Revisit them often. Use them as a lens to view your thoughts, actions, and relationships.

There's a reason why *Emotional Enlightenment* feels so elusive to most people. It's not something you achieve by looking outside yourself. The world will tell you that peace is somewhere out there, just beyond your reach. But the truth? You can't buy it, earn it, or find it in someone else's approval. Peace is what's left when you stop searching. It's been within you all along.

The **Eight Keys** were never about fixing you, because you don't need fixing—they were about helping you peel back the layers of fear, anger, sadness, hurt, guilt, and shame that kept you from seeing the truth. The truth that **you've always been whole.** The truth that your worth has never depended on what you've done or what's been done to you.

Emotional Enlightenment isn't some mystical state reserved for the enlightened few. It's practical. It's real. And it's closer than you think.

The Stories We Tell Ourselves

Let me pull back the veil and show you what life was like for me before I discovered this work. I wasn't just reactive—I was a ticking time bomb, ready to explode at the smallest spark. I had a good heart buried somewhere under all the chaos, but you wouldn't have seen it. The world I lived in, the world I created for myself, was one of constant tension, anger, and distrust.

I faced molestation and abuse as a kid. I grew up feeling like I had to fight to survive, and somewhere along the way, that fight turned inward. I became my own worst enemy. I was a drunk, a womanizer, and an abuser—not because I wanted to be, but because I didn't know another way to cope with the pain. My relationships were a mess because I didn't trust anyone, and honestly, I didn't trust myself.

Steroids and caffeine fueled my days, keeping me wired and on edge. My mind created dangers that didn't exist, and my body stayed ready for battles that would never come. The anger? That was my armor. It made me feel in control when everything inside me screamed the opposite.

I treated my parents like less than human beings, even though they deserved better. I lived my life as if the world owed me something while carrying the unbearable weight of believing I wasn't enough. By the time I was 20, I'd experienced more trauma than most people face in a lifetime. I should've been dead, in prison, or strung out on some drug. Instead, I'm living proof of what's possible.

The truth is, the pain I carried wasn't just about what happened to me—it was about the meanings I attached to those events. For me, those meanings sounded like:

"Women who love me will leave me."

"I'm not good enough."

"I'll never be loved."

"I'm a fraud."

Those stories ran my life. Every decision, every reaction, every relationship was filtered through those beliefs. I didn't even realize it at the time, but those thoughts were shaping my reality.

However, your mind can't hold onto a positive understanding and a negative emotion at the same time. It's like trying to see the sun while staring at a storm cloud. The negative emotions cloud your vision, keeping you stuck in the pain and preventing you from seeing the truth.

When I started to do this work—when I really allowed myself to reflect on those stories—I saw them for what they were: lies. Lies I told myself to make sense of a world that didn't make sense to me as a kid. The pain I carried wasn't a reflection of who I was; it was a reflection of what I'd been through. And as I began to let go of those emotions, the clouds cleared, and the truth started to shine through.

Imagine an emotional cup inside of you. Every time you experience anger, sadness, fear, hurt, or guilt, a drop gets added to that cup. The first time you feel those emotions as a kid, your mind puts a stopper in the bottom of the cup, holding onto those drops.

And the truth is, life doesn't stop. More drops keep coming. By the time you're an adult, that cup is overflowing. And when it's full, you're not just reacting to what's happening in the moment—you're reacting to everything that's ever filled that cup.

For instance, have you ever snapped at someone over something small, only to realize later that it wasn't about them? That's an example of your emotional cup spilling over. It's not the moment that triggers you; it's the weight of everything you've been carrying.

For me, my cup was filled to the brim. Every outburst, every destructive choice, every time I pushed someone away—it wasn't about them. It was about the overflow. And I didn't realize it until I went inward, faced myself and started emptying that cup.

All that anger, sadness, fear, and guilt you've been carrying isn't just baggage—it's dormant wisdom waiting to be unlocked. But you can't see the wisdom until you release the emotion. Your mind can't hold onto both at the same time.

When I revisited those memories—really looked at them, not through the lens of anger but through the lens of curiosity—I saw something I'd never seen before. I saw the lessons. I saw the patterns. I saw the wisdom buried beneath the pain.

I realized that the anger I carried wasn't just anger—it was a shield I used to protect myself from feeling vulnerable. The guilt wasn't just guilt—it was a misguided attempt to hold myself accountable for things I couldn't control. The sadness wasn't just sadness—it was my heart's way of asking for help.

As I let go of those emotions, the pain dissolved, and the memories stopped hurting. They didn't disappear, but they no longer defined me. They became just that—memories. And the wisdom they held? That stayed.

If you'd met me back then, you'd never guess that I'd end up here. Living the life of my dreams. Free from the anger that used to consume me. Trusting people in ways I never thought I could. Loving in ways I didn't think were possible.

This isn't theory. This isn't just something I read in a book. This is my life. Let me repeat it again, *Emotional Enlightenment* isn't some mystical state reserved for the lucky few—it's practical, it's real, and it's available to you.

But here's the catch, freedom isn't free. *Emotional Enlightenment*, as incredible and life-changing as it is, comes with a cost. And the cost isn't financial. It's deeper. It's emotional. It takes courage. You have to be willing to do the work. You have to be willing to open the closet and look at the things you've been avoiding for years, maybe decades. You have to be willing to feel what you've been numbing for years and sit with your pain, not as a victim, but as a student. And that's no small task. That's the cost of freedom. And it's worth every ounce of effort.

Here's what I want you to remember, the cost of freedom is temporary. The cost of staying stuck lasts forever.

Opening the Closet

Think about the things you've shoved into the back of your emotional closet. The betrayals you never processed. The anger you've been holding onto. The guilt and shame that still whisper in the back of your mind. For years, you've been slamming that door shut, hoping that if you ignore it long enough, it'll just go away. But it doesn't.

That closet doesn't stay shut—it leaks. It spills into your thoughts, your reactions, your relationships. It shapes the way you see the world and the way you see yourself. And until you open that door, until you face what's inside, you can't be free.

I know it sounds terrifying. Opening that door means letting yourself feel emotions you've spent your whole life running from. It means being vulnerable in a way that might feel unbearable at first. But to be real, that vulnerability is not a weakness. It's a doorway.

When you open that closet and face what's inside, you don't just release the weight—you reclaim your life. You get to experience the world without the filter of past pain. You get to show up in your relationships with openness and love instead of fear and resentment. You get to create a future that isn't dictated by your past.

What's the cost of staying stuck? Of holding onto the anger, the fear, the sadness, the guilt, the hurt and the shame? Because make no mistake—there's a cost to that, too.

Think about the relationships you've lost because you couldn't let go of resentment. Think about the opportunities you've missed because fear held you back. Think about the joy you've robbed yourself of because you couldn't see past the pain.

When you stay stuck, you don't just pay the price in your emotions—you pay it in your life. You carry the weight of old stories into every new chapter. You stay trapped in cycles that keep you from the freedom you deserve.

The work of *Emotional Enlightenment* is hard, but staying stuck? That's harder.

I'm not asking you to forget what happened to you. I'm not asking you to pretend the pain wasn't real. I'm asking you to let go of the stories that keep you chained to it.

Letting go doesn't mean you lose the lesson—it means you lose the weight. You keep the wisdom, the understanding, the strength, but you release the anger, the fear, the guilt.

You see, the thing about letting go is it's not a one-time decision. It's a daily practice. Every time you feel that old emotion rise up, you have a choice. You can cling to it, or you can release it.

Freedom isn't something you achieve once and for all. It's something you choose, moment by moment, day by day. And with each choice, it gets a little easier.

A Worthwhile Investment

The cost of freedom might feel steep in the moment, but the return on investment? It's priceless. Some days will feel effortless. Others will feel like a struggle. But every step you take brings you closer to the truth of who you are—a being of infinite peace, wisdom, and love. When you commit to this work, you're not just changing how you feel—you're changing how you live.

You're giving yourself the gift of peace, clarity, and presence. You're creating a life where you're no longer defined by your past but empowered by it.

And here's the most beautiful part: every step you take on this journey inspires others to take their own. When you show up as someone who's free, who's *Emotionally Enlightened*, you give others permission to do the same.

So, yes, there's a cost to freedom. But what you gain in return—a life of peace, joy, and possibility—is worth every ounce of effort. So, take it one moment at a time, one choice at a time. Trust the process. And know that the freedom you're seeking is already within you, waiting to be uncovered.

Invitation to Go Deeper

By now, you've walked a journey that many people never even begin. You've faced the stories you've told yourself, uncovered the beliefs that shaped your life, and gained tools to create the emotional freedom you deserve. This book has been a guide, a companion on your path, but I want to remind you of something: this is just the beginning.

The truth is, no book—no matter how powerful—can compare to experiencing transformation in real time, in the presence of others who are walking the same path, and know you're not alone. When you share your story, not only do you begin to heal, but you also give others permission to heal too. There's something about being in a room, sharing your heart, and seeing someone else's breakthrough that makes this work feel alive. It's no longer just words on a page; it's something you feel in your soul.

This isn't about me or any guru at the front of the room. This is about you finding your own answers, your own truth. My role is simply to guide you back to yourself, to hold up a mirror so you can see the beauty and wholeness that's always been there.

I remember a retreat not too long ago where a woman—I'll call her Sarah—came in carrying years of guilt and shame. She had spent her life believing she was never enough, that every mistake she'd made defined her. She sat quietly the first day, holding back tears, unsure if this work could really help her. But as the days unfolded, something shifted.

When we walked through the **Eight Keys** together, she revisited a memory from her childhood, one that had haunted her for years. And in that moment, she saw it differently. She realized it wasn't her fault. She wasn't broken. And for the first time, she forgave herself.

I'll never forget the look on her face as she let out a breath she'd been holding for decades. It was like watching someone step into the light after living in darkness for so long. By the end of the retreat, Sarah wasn't just lighter—she was radiant. She left knowing she was enough, she was already whole just as she was, and ready to live her life from a place of peace and freedom.

The Next Step

You don't have to do this alone. Whether it's revisiting the chapters of this book, attending a live session, or joining us for a retreat, there are so many ways to deepen this work.

Maybe you've been reading this book and thinking, "I'm not sure if I'm ready." Let me tell you this, you don't have to be ready. You just have to be willing. Willing to look within. Willing to take one step forward. Willing to believe, even for a moment, that emotional freedom is possible for you.

The retreats, workshops, and live sessions I offer aren't about fixing you—they're about giving you the space to remember the truth. And the truth is **you are already whole**. They're about taking the tools and keys you've discovered here and putting them into practice in a way that feels real, tangible, and life-changing.

Before you close this book, I want you to pause for a moment and reflect on everything you've uncovered. You've come so far, and yet this is just the start of what's possible.

You have the tools. You have the keys. You have the wisdom.

Now it's up to you to keep walking this path. Whether you continue on your own, revisit the chapters, or join us in a live experience, know this: you are capable of creating a life of peace, freedom, and *Emotional Enlightenment*.

The only question is—what's your next step? Whatever it is, know that I'm here cheering you on, every step of the way.

If you're ready to go deeper, to experience the **Eight Keys** live, or to join a retreat, I would be honored to walk this journey with you. Together, we can create the space for transformation, for healing, and for the freedom you've always deserved.

The journey doesn't end here—it begins here. Visit www.the8keys.com

Take the step. You're worth it.

Conclusion

Your New Journey Begins Here

Take a moment. **Breathe.** Let this all sink in.

You've done something most people never do. You've made space for deep reflection, for truth, for remembering. If you've made it this far, it tells me something about you:

You're ready.

Ready to live differently. Ready to let go of old stories. Ready to meet yourself fully, without the weight of who you thought you had to be.

I know we've never met, but I need you to hear me when I say this. I see you. Not the version of you shaped by survival. Not the roles you've played or the masks you've worn.

I see the real you. The you beneath all the fear, doubt, and old habits. The you that is whole, untouched, and unbreakable. You don't need to become someone new. **There's nothing missing. There's nothing to fix.** But stepping into that truth? That's the journey.

This isn't about getting everything "right." Life will still bring challenges. You will still face hard days. But now, you know how to meet those moments differently—with awareness, with choice, with freedom.

The **Eight Keys** aren't just ideas. They are tools. They are your roadmap back to yourself. Some days, everything will click. Other days, it will feel messy. That's okay. This isn't about perfection—it's about practice. When you forget, come back to the **Eight Keys**. When life feels heavy, come back to the truth: **You are already enough.**

Every moment is an invitation to begin again.

An Invitation Just for You

I don't want you to walk this path alone.

If something in these pages has woken something inside you—if you feel like you're on the edge of a breakthrough but don't know what comes next—you don't have to figure it out alone.

This work comes alive when it's shared. There's something powerful about being in a space with others who are doing the same deep inner work.

If you feel called to take this journey further—to experience the **Eight Keys** live, to go deeper, to truly integrate this work into your life—there are ways to do that. Whether it's a coaching session, a workshop, or a retreat, these principles are designed to meet you where you are and guide you forward. Visit: www.The8keys.com

And if you ever need someone to bring this to your team, community, or organization, I'm here for that too.

This isn't just something I teach. **This is something I live.**

You Are Already Whole

Before we part ways, there's one last thing I need you to know.

You are already enough.

Right now. In this moment. Not *once you heal more*. Not *once you fix something about yourself*. Not *once you achieve more*. The peace, love, and freedom you've been searching for? They've been inside you all along.

You've always been whole.

I know it's easy to forget that. The world will try to convince you otherwise. It will tell you that you need more, that you must do more, that something is missing.

But I'm here to remind you nothing is missing. You don't need to strive or struggle to become someone else. The only thing left to do is be yourself—fully, freely, without fear. Not because you need love in return, but because **you are love itself.**

This is not the end.

This is the beginning.

There's a whole life ahead of you—one filled with joy, freedom, and possibility. It won't always be easy, but you now have the tools to meet life as it comes. And when things get hard remember, you've got this.

You've already done the hardest part—you've opened yourself up to the truth. Now, it's time to live from that truth. To wake up each day with curiosity, playfulness, and trust. To give love freely, without fear. And to know—without a doubt—that you are enough.

I'm rooting for you. I believe in you. And if you ever need a reminder, just know I'm here. I'm ready when you are. You are already everything you've ever needed to be. Now, it's time to live like it.

With all my love,
Elijah

P.S. I want to hear from you!
This book was never meant to be a one-way conversation. If something in these pages spoke to you—if a shift happened, if a breakthrough unfolded, if you saw yourself in a new way—I would love to hear your story.

You can reach me directly at Elijah@belieftheory.com

Tell me what resonated. Tell me what changed. Tell me what's still unfolding. Your journey matters. Your voice matters. And I'm honored to be a part of it.

I look forward to hearing from you.

Made in the USA
Coppell, TX
17 February 2026

71642285R00136